EVEN COARSER RUGBY

N.N.

Also in Arrow by Michael Green

THE ART OF COARSE ACTING
THE ART OF COARSE GOLF
THE ART OF COARSE RUGBY
THE ART OF COARSE DRINKING
THE ART OF COARSE SAILING
THE ART OF COARSE SEX

EVEN COARSER RUGBY

or

What Did You Do to Ronald?

Michael Green

Illustrated by Haro

ARROW BOOKS

Arrow Books Limited
17–21 Conway Street, London W1P 6JD

An imprint of the Hutchinson Publishing Group

London Melbourne Sydney Auckland
Johannesburg and agencies throughout
the world

First published by Hutchinson 1963

Arrow edition 1969

New edition 1985

Set in Baskerville by Rowland Phototypesetting Limited
Bury St Edmunds, Suffolk

Printed and bound in Great Britain by
Anchor Brendon Limited, Tiptree, Essex

ISBN 0 09 943460 1

Contents

Introduction

When *The Art of Coarse Rugby* was published back in 1960 I naturally thought I'd exhausted the subject of rugby's lower depths, but I soon found how wrong I was. Within days of publication an old friend rang up to say, 'Mike, you forgot to put in about that time you played opposite a man with a steel plate in his skull and the opposing skipper asked you not to tackle him too hard in case he dropped dead.' In fact fresh material kept accumulating all the time, some of which I incorporated in further articles and broadcasts. In 1963 these were collected and published under the title *Even Coarser Rugby*. But there was still more to come, and later additional material was published by Pelham Books and Sphere as *Michael Green's Rugby Alphabet*.

In this new version of *Even Coarser Rugby* I have combined some pieces from both books and added new material, as well as disposing of some bits which didn't stand the test of time, thus creating what is, I hope, an improved successor to *Coarse Rugby*. As this is still in print after 25 years I feel there should still be room for the sequel. I am grateful to the *Sunday Times*, the *Observer*, *Punch* and the *Rugby World* for the use of my articles which originally appeared in those publications.

Although I have made many alterations, I haven't

attempted to bring all the contributions up-to-date. To start with, with the rugby scene changes so swiftly these days that any changes could themselves be outdated quickly. And although the period flavour of old money, baggy trousers and gramophones at club dances may seem old-fashioned, human nature doesn't change. I hope therefore that the spirit of the older pieces still stands up, even though some were written when there were 240 pence to the pound and you were forbidden to pick up the ball after a tackle. I remember the first game after the law changed in 1959. The first player to take advantage of the new law and pick up the ball was penalized, and when he said to the ref, 'What about the new laws?' the ref replied, 'What new laws?'

Of course, not everything remains the same. Hotel-wrecking by rugby teams, which used to be just a merry Easter jape, has become unacceptable hooliganism. But the best tour pranks were not vandalistic and could be quite funny. My own most vivid memory is when the Northampton team, whom I was accompanying as a reporter, removed my trousers in the train and flung them out of the window, whence they were last seen decorating the front of an express going in the opposite direction at 100 mph. At Liverpool I succeeded in getting to the hotel in my overcoat and tried to come down to dinner dressed in pyjama trousers. All might have been well, but I was spotted by Don White, the Northampton skipper, who called over the head waiter and said I was some sort of nut-case who used to follow the team around in pyjamas. 'He's quite harmless, really,' he said, 'but we would be glad if you'd not allow him in the dining-room, because he is an embarrassment to us. He may start shouting and tear off his clothes at any minute.' I was firmly escorted outside by the head waiter and told they would send something up to my room.

With sport, including rugby, becoming more and more commercialized, perhaps it's a good thing to be reminded occasionally that it's all supposed to be for fun really, not an extension of the advertising industry. On the day when sportsmen can't laugh at themselves it will be time to pack it all in.

Michael Green
London, 1985

1

When Blood on a Postcard is Significant

One of the great mysteries of rugby football is: what makes a man become team secretary? Most administrative positions do at least involve a certain amount of power; even secretaries and treasurers are allowed to write rude letters to people who don't pay their subs or who set fire to opponents' pavilions. But the team secretary is merely the passive recipient of a torrent of evasion and abuse, a sort of pillar-box for rude communications, who's not entitled to answer back.

It is true, at the top of the tree, there must be a certain satisfaction in sending out a lofty summons to play for Harlequins against Cardiff, especially if you get a phone call back to say the recipient has broken a bone in his foot but will desperately try to get fit as he doesn't want to lose his place. But that sort of situation is rare for the average team secretary. He is much more likely to have the postcard returned (unstamped) with '— off' scrawled all over it. That is always assuming there isn't some pathetic excuse like, 'Must be a mistake, you know I never turn out against Finchley as it involves changing trains . . .'

In some mysterious way, people who drop out after selection always seem to manage to make it appear the team secretary's fault. Every entrenched and suppressed piece of venom and hatred is directed at that innocent

individual simply because his signature happens to be on
the bottom of the card. Men with a grievance, who are
content merely to mutter in the clubhouse, will burst out
against a team secretary, often scrawling completely
irrelevant graffiti when they return their cards, or dia-
tribes such as, 'Am not available as long as the club
persists in charging a pound for hot dogs . . .'

Yet there are always people willing to do the job. My
own theory is that they take it on because they have a
deep-rooted desire to be needed. And, by golly, they are.

Theoretically, of course, a team secretary's duties are
merely to note the selection committee decisions on
Monday evening, and send out cards to those picked.
These are usually couched in the sternest language,
informing the recipient that if he scratches after noon on
Wednesday he will instantly be expelled from the club.

In practice, however, that is but the start of the team
secretary's troubles. He usually finishes up by personally
selecting four-fifths of the players in anything up to
half-a-dozen sides. Far from doing this in calm consideration during the week, the whole process has to be tele-
scoped into an insane period between eight o'clock on
Friday evening (the favourite time for dropping out of
rugby teams) and three o'clock on Saturday afternoon. He
may well still be at it right up to half-time, trying to
persuade a coach-driver to play. The team secretary
himself is expected to fill the last gap if under forty-five.

The situation in the average team secretary's home on
a Friday evening needs a skilled administrative staff of five
to cope with it. Instead, there is one man, aided perhaps
by a few members of his family, which leads to the
ridiculous situation that half the Extra B's in this country
are selected by someone's wife or mother, or even the
German au pair girl.

Indeed, I recollect my old club losing its unbeaten
record because the team secretary was in the bathroom
when the stand-off rang to say he couldn't play. His aged

mother took the call, and although I forget what the player's real name was, I do know she wrote it down as 'Guggenheim'.

Faced with a message saying, 'Mr Guggenheim can't play', the team secretary decided that anyone with a name like that must be in the fifth team, and ordered his last stand-by (an elderly cripple of about fifty-five) to substitute. The result was that, for the first time in living memory, the C XV had sixteen players, while the first team had to play the touch-judge, with disastrous results.

The following dialogue must not be uncommon on Friday evenings:

Team Secretary: Sorry I'm late, darling. I was kept at the office . . . well, I did just have half a pint on the way home. Any calls?

Wife: About fourteen. Smelly Smith has gone to Hong Kong. Dai Evans, Idris Morgan and Ivor Jones have all been struck by a sudden disease. Fred Fogg, Alf Jordan, Bert Smith and Weevil Watson are all injured; Jigger, Knocker, Chalky, Dusty and Nobby can't play; Arthur Wright is getting divorced, and Tom Brown won't play.

Team Secretary: Won't?

Wife: Yes. He says he distinctly told you after the same game last season that they were the dirtiest crowd he'd ever met, and he'd never play them again. He says he can't understand why you didn't remember, and if this is the way the club's run, no wonder it's got such a rotten playing record.

Team Secretary: What have you done?

Wife: I picked out the first fourteen names from that list of yours and phoned them to play.

Team Secretary: My God! That's the list of people not allowed to play until they pay their subscription.

Wife: It doesn't matter. Only three said they'd turn out. By the way, you'll need some new laces in your boots. I put you down for the Extra A.

The state into which a team secretary is reduced is frequently revealed by the condition of a match card sent to a player. These contain valuable clues. The presence of blood on a match card, for instance, means it was written during breakfast after the sender had cut himself shaving, and the recipient, therefore, is a last-minute choice.

Tea cup rings indicate the secretary's wife sent it, a sign that the player concerned is a substitute for someone else. Beer stains are an indication one is an original selection. They are caused during the selection committee meeting, as the team secretary scribbles away with a pint at his elbow.

Sometimes, of course, the match cards don't arrive at all, as on the occasion when our team secretary's wife, having been given the cards to post, carried them around in the car for a week, with the result not one player out of seventy-five turned up on Saturday. I think this particular official must have been prone to bad luck because on another occasion his dog ate the entire First XV front-row.

However, I did once receive a card which revealed such extraordinary confusion that I kept it as a souvenir and an example of the state to which a team secretary can be reduced.

To start with, there was a scorch mark across one corner, a nail varnish stain and a pencilled note: 'Get cat food.'

It began 'Dear Fred'. This was crossed out and 'Dear Bert' substituted, but this was also crossed out in favour of 'Dear Mike'.

It continued: 'You have been selected to play on Saturday for . . .' and on the dotted line was written, 'Either the First XV, the Extra A or the Extra C.' This extraordinary statement was explained by a little footnote which said, 'Please meet at the Baker's Arms at one o'clock and if the First XV do not have a stand-off be prepared to travel to High Wycombe. But if Frank Matthews returns from

Manchester, please pick up Charlie Brown at the corner
of Hanger Lane, and play for the Extra C provided that
Sid Hawkins does not contact you as full-back for the
Extra A.'

. As a final insult there was scrawled across the bottom
the stock warning 'Please be fit for this important fixture.'

In the end the First XV lost 48–nil. Not that I was
there. I was intercepted at the pub door with an urgent
message to pick up Jack Robinson at Kew Bridge and
proceed at once to Salisbury, where the fourth team had
already gone by coach. It was dark when we arrived.

2

For Three Points and a Peanut

(This account of my excursion to an international in Paris was written in 1958. It shows how much has changed since then – and how much hasn't.)

'Of course, you know only half of them go to the match?' said the tubby little man as the bar of the *Normannia* sawed up and down. We were at sea on British Rail's cheap excursion to Paris for the rugby international.

'I book up every time. Got my ticket in December. I do some business in the morning and see some friends in the evening. Wouldn't go near the game if you paid me.'

It seemed he might be right. The train from Waterloo had contained some most unlikely-looking rugger types, from nine-year-old girls to bearded professional hitch-hikers in waterproof jackets. But as the boat plunged on it became clear that there must be some rugger players at least on board. Huddled miserably in the heaving gang-way by the gents' lavatory (every time anyone rushed in to be sick they trod all over me), I caught snatches of familiar song from the bar, about a little baby called Stephen who was born under unusual circumstances.

The *Normannia*'s saloon looked like the inside of a troop train, with sleepers tumbled all over it in fantastic positions. At 3 a.m. someone trod on my face and announced he had drunk a bottle of whisky. A few steps further on he fell flat on his face and bellowed for help in a Scots accent. His friends sensibly declined and he spent the rest of the night muttering hideous obscenities. Even the singers were silent now.

A bleary-eyed crowd stumbled on to the train at Le Havre. Three blessed hours of sleep and warmth, and then Paris and a queue to shave in cold water. A shabby Frenchman took twenty-five minutes over an elaborate toilet ritual in front of a queue of impatient Englishmen.

'Come on, you stupid old geezer. Try standing nearer the razor.'

'*Merci, m'sieur.*'

'*Merci* yourself.'

I gave up and looked for a taxi to the *Observer* office. I had a phrase-book of the-postilion-has-been-struck-by-lightning type, but it didn't tell you how to talk to deaf taxi-drivers, so I found myself at the other end of Paris. When I tried to explain the driver made a noise as if he was being sick, which I couldn't translate, so I caught the Métro.

There was a lovely compartment at the end of the carriage with several empty seats, although the train was packed, so I gratefully sat down. After a moment or two I realized everyone was staring at me. It appeared I was sitting by a notice saying that the empty seats were reserved for *mutilés de la guerre* and pregnant women. Not only was I undamaged in the war but I was not pregnant.

There was only one thing to do. Stiffening a leg to give the impression it was artificial, I stumped down the carriage and with the greatest difficulty descended at the next stop. I hope they all felt ashamed.

At the *Observer* office they said they had not got me a ticket. Frankly, I think they had, but they refused to believe I was from the *Observer*. I didn't blame them when I saw reflected in a shop window a blotched, unshaven figure crowned by what appeared to be the business end of

a mop and clutching a London Co-operative Society
carrier bag.

No time to worry. Back to Saint-Lazare for the train to
Colombes. There was an electric train starting as I ran on
to the platform and I managed to jump on the running-
board as it moved off. Then I wished I hadn't.

Inside they were packed so tightly that I couldn't pull
the sliding doors apart. I clung to the handles, my face
pressed against the glass about a quarter of an inch from a
cynical Frenchman in a beret who returned my stare with
a singular lack of concern. The train accelerated to 150
mph. At least it felt like 150, although it might have been
slightly slower. It is not easy to judge when you are
standing outside the carriage.

'*M'aider*,' I squeaked feebly. '*M'aider. Je suis in peril of mort
horrible.*' In the distance another train was approaching.
Mort stared me in the face.

'*Je ne veux pas to die*,' I shouted. 'Permit me to enter
myself in the *porte tout suite*.'

Some Anglophile inside forced the door open six inches
and grunted '*Allez-vous-en*'[1] unemotionally. I squeezed in
and was greeted by a whiff of garlic. It smelt like the
flowers of heaven in my state. I looked in the phrase-book
for a section 'On Escaping From Death', but there was
nothing to meet the situation, not even 'Kindly tell the
postilion I am extremely grateful to him for saving my
life.' All I could find was 'Have we to get out for the
Customs examination?'

There was no trouble getting a ticket at Colombes. A
tout outside the station waved one in my face (a ticket –
not a station). I wanted to sit down under cover, so I
insisted: '*Je me veux couver*,' and he nodded, which showed
some restraint, as I was apparently saying: 'I wish to
incubate myself.' He wanted 5,000 old francs for the
ticket. I offered 2,000 and he accepted with alacrity. I

[1] This means 'Get out!' Obviously I misheard.

wondered why until I saw that the price on the ticket was 250.

Another man came up, wished me luck and pinned a Union Jack in my lapel. I started to thank him. 'No thanks,' he said. 'Four hundred francs. Good luck.'

The English at the stadium were conspicuous by the fact that they were all drinking bottled beer and talking loudly. Some of them seemed to have been drinking beer ever since they left England. One wore the legend 'Olympic Drinking Champion' on his back. Several wore City dress of striped trousers and bowlers.

I did not see the game under the best circumstances, as my ticket was in the worst possible part of the ground. I was also near a group of English supporters who sang dirty songs under the mistaken impression that the French didn't understand them. In shame I turned up my collar and tried to look French, occasionally muttering phrases like *'Aux armes, mes braves'* and *'Formez vos battalions . . .'*

For a nation with one of the highest number of alcoholics in Europe the French drinking facilities at Colombes are small, especially compared with those at Twickenham, but the English contingent managed to fill themselves up. Two hours after the game (which I believe ended in a 3–3 draw) groups of lurching figures were weaving towards the station, some carrying Tricolours and Union Jacks. Two men, one in a kilt, were going round in circles aimlessly.

'I'm not drunk, Jock,' explained one. 'I'm just waltzing.'

There was a good deal of shouting outside the Café de la Gare, where a middle-aged man kept demanding to know where the women were. Inside the café two stolid Englishmen of about forty were drinking beer and bought one for me.

Two hours later we had gone on to red wine and had been joined by a villainous-looking French peanut vendor, whom we had to conciliate after I threw a bag of peanuts at him (he was overcharging outrageously). After the fourth glass of our wine the peanut man said he was a Communist and started a violent row over politics with one of the Englishmen, which ended with both of them making for the door in a hostile attitude.

As red wine was just about coming out of our ears by now, we didn't realize what was happening until we found that the whole café had walked out with them. 'Bobby is in trouble,' said my companion magnificently. 'We must help him.' This sounded fine until we got outside and saw that the street was deserted. Only the noise of raised voices from another bar guided us to where Bobby and the peanut man were bandying insults. By now they had reached the stage of drunkenly pushing each other in the chest. It was time to interfere.

'We must act,' said my friend firmly. 'Hey, you there, *homme de* peanut. Give me your tie and I will give you mine. That is a sign of friendship in England.'

Bobby translated and the Frenchman handed over a

filthy, greasy object, red of course, and attached to elastic Dicky put it on and exchanged his rugger club tie, very English and very expensive.

The peanut man took it, threw it on the floor and spat on it.

I have never seen anyone more hurt than the Englishman. 'I say,' he complained. 'That's not English, you know. We don't do that sort of thing.'

The peanut vendor spat again. He walked to the door and spat. Then he went into the street and spat. I wouldn't swear it, but I think he spat as he went past the window. We never saw him again.

Events are blurred after that. I vaguely remember a nightmare journey and then it was dawn and I was lying on the deck of the *Normannia*, chattering with cold. A gnome with a small pick was trying to dig a trench across my forehead. My mouth felt like the inside of a bus-driver's glove.

I had a strong feeling of unease. What had happened the night before? Did I really meet two Englishmen and have a row with a Communist peanut vendor? I couldn't believe it.

Something crunched underneath me. I felt in my pocket.

It was a peanut.

3

UN OBSERVATEUR ANGLAIS AUTORISE:
An English reporter:

Vêtus de Bérets Basques, les
Wearing   *Basque*   *berets,*   *the*

Français Vivent de Rapines, d'ail
French   *live*   *by*   *plunder,*   *garlic*

et de Cacahuètes
and   *peanuts*

BY YVAN AUDOUARD

This article appeared in the French Newspaper *Paris-Presse* in
reply to my account of the Paris trip. I am indebted to its
author, M. Yvan Audouard, for permission to reproduce it.
The translation, as will be obvious, is by me. Personally, I
think it's funnier than the original.

M. Michael Green, dont les fonctions semblent être celles
Mr. Michael Green, whose functions appear to be those

de reporter au journal britannique 'The Observer' fut chargé,
of a reporter on the British newspaper 'The Observer', was charged

la semaine dernière, de la délicate mission de visiter Paris, et
last week, with the delicate mission of visiting Paris, and

d'en rendre compte, sous le fallacieux prétexte du match de
giving an account under the fallacious pretext of the

rugby France-Angleterre.
French-English rugby match.

Après une traversée qui, selon ses propres dires, avait été
After a crossing which, in his own words, was

copieusement arrosée de nombreuses rasades de whisky,
copiously   sprinkled with   numerous   bumpers of   whisky,

M. Green arriva à Paris dans un état de décrépitude avancée
Mr. Green arrived in Paris in a state of   advanced decrepitude

et (dit-il) de 'saleté repoussante'.
and (says he)   'repulsively dirty'.

Les toilettes de la gare étaient pleines de Français indifférents
The toilets at the station were   full of   indifferent

et goguenards qui, probablement ligués pour on ne sait quelles
and jeering Frenchmen who, probably ganging-up for I don't know what

raisons, lui interdirent l'accès au moindre petit lavabo.
reasons, forbade him   access to the   wash-basin.

Sortant de la gare, il sauta dans un taxi, jeta au chauffeur
Leaving   the station, he jumped into a taxi and hurled at the driver

l'adresse du bureau parisien de 'The Observer'. Or, non
the address of the Paris office of 'The Observer'. But, not

seulement la chauffeur n'avait pas compris, mais il était sourd
only   didn't the driver   understand,   but he was deaf

(probablement un peu aveugle aussi) et notre malheureux
(probably   a little blind as well) and our   unfortunate

Britannique se retrouva a l'autre bout de Paris. Il paya et
Britisher   found himself at the other end of Paris. He paid and

demanda au chauffeur, la voix étranglée, ce qu'il devait faire.
asked the driver,   in a choked voice, what he ought to do.

L'autre se contenta de grogner un mot incompréhensible, puis,
The driver contented himself with grunting an   incomprehensible word, then,

superbement indifférent, embraya.
superbly   indifferent, drove off.

M. Green prit alors le métro. C'était—bien entendu—l'heure
Mr. Green then took the métro. It was —naturally—   rush-

de pointe.
hour.

Dans le compartiment, surchargé de travailleurs éreintés,
In the compartment,   packed   with tired travellers,

quatre banquettes étaient libres. Il s'y installa, mais ne
four   seats   were   free. He installed himself there, but

s'aperçut que plus tard, le malheureux, qu'une pancarte
did not perceive until too late, the unfortunate fact that there was a notice

indiquait clairement que ces sièges, étaient réserves aux
indicating   clearly   that the seats   were   reserved for the

mutilés et aux femmes enceintes. Les Français ne les occupaient
wounded and for   pregnant women.   The   French   did not occupy

pas, respectueux comme chacun le sait de la loi, quelle qu'elle
them,   respectful   of the law,   such   as it is.

soit. Aussi, c'est sous une volée d'injures et de regards haineux
So,   it was under a   shower of insults and   hateful looks

que M. Green, démoralisé, sortit du métro.
that Mr. Green,   demoralized,   left   the métro.

Au bureau de 'The Observer' et pour des raisons assez
At   'The Observer' office,   and for   reasons rather

obscures, on refusa de luis donner un billet d'entree pour le
obscure, they refused to   give him a   ticket   for the

match. Sans verser une seule larme sur son sort, M. Green,
game. Without shedding a single   tear   on his fate, Mr. Green,

héroïque, repartit (à pied, cette fois) vers la gare Saint-Lazare.
heroic,   returned (on foot, this time)   to Saint-Lazare station.

Le train pour Colombes démarrait à cet instant precis. Les
The train for   Colombes   was leaving at that   very moment.   The

portières automatiques étaient déjà fermées. N'écoutant que
automatic doors   were already closed.   Listening only to

son courage, il sauta sur le marche-pied. Le train prenuit de la
his courage, he jumped on the running-board. The train speeded up.

vitesse. M. Green, ignoré du monde entier, était toujours sur
Mr. Green,   ignored by the whole world,   was nevertheless on

le marche-pied accroché aux barres d'accès. Son regard était
the running-board, clinging to the door handles. His look was

suppliant, si suppliant, qu'un Français (cynique et le chef
suppliant, so suppliant that a Frenchman (cynical and his main

coiffé, comme quarante cinq millions d'autres Français, d'un
headgear, like   45   million   other Frenchmen, a

béret basque) entrouvrit la portière et murmura calmement:
Basque beret),   opened   the   door and murmured   calmly:

'Allez-vous en!'
'Go away!'

M. Green sourit humblement, forca l'interstice et pénétra
Mr. Green smiled   humbly,   forced   the gap and penetrated

dans le wagon.
into the carriage.

Là, une gigantesque bouffée d'ail l'assallit et envahit ses
There, a great whiff of garlic attacked him and invaded his

narines.
nostrils.

A Colombes, il fallait touver un billet. Un quidam lui en
At Colombes, he had to find a ticket. Someone offered

proposa un, pour 5,000 anciens francs. M. Green marchanda,
him one for 5,000 old francs. Mr. Green bargained,

l'obtint à 2,000 francs, et s'aperçut un peu plus tard, que le
got it for 2,000 francs, and perceived a little later that the

prix du billet était de 250 francs.
price of the ticket was 250 francs.

Le match se déroula sans encombre, pendant que M. Green,
The game went on without interruption, during which Mr. Green,

saisi d'une activité fébrile, buvait du vin rouge et de la bière, se
seized with feverish activity, drank red wine and beer,

fasait prendre à partie par un marchand de cacahuètes voleur et
was forced into a quarrel with a peanut seller (thief and

communiste, un marchand d'insignes, voleur et sans opinion
communist), a flag seller (thief and without

politique déterminée, et plusiers spectateurs voleurs et agressifs.
resolute political opinion), and a lot of spectators (thieves and aggressive).

Las de sa faire rouler par la France entière, M. Green
Weary of being swindled by all France, Mr. Green

repartit pour Londres le soir même, nanti d'une solide migraine
left for London the same evening, provided with a bad headache

et d'une bouche un peu pâteuse . . .
and a nasty taste in his mouth . . .

4

How to Tackle Men of Superior Rank

The edict by the Army Sports Council that military sportsmen must stop calling each other by first names and use ranks instead will bring a nostalgic glow to millions of war-time squaddies and national servicemen. It is obvious the council are anxious to return to the days of the conscript army when soldiers would be given the choice between playing rugby or cleaning out the latrines, and frequently chose the latrines. It's a shame really, because matters had improved so much since and Service sport is today far removed from the farce it sometimes used to be when we stood firm against the Hun and various other enemies. I use the word farce advisedly. Where else in rugby would a player shout, 'I order you to stop pulling my testicles'?

I shan't easily forget the first time I realized sport in the Services was different from elsewhere. It was 1944 and I'd been in the Army a fortnight when my name appeared in orders for fire picket. On the next page my name appeared in the unit rugby team for a match. Both events commenced at the same time.

I spoke to the sergeant, who said the penalty for not parading on fire picket was death. I spoke to Lieutenant Bird, who ran the rugby side, and he said the penalty for not playing rugby when ordered to do so was also death.

So I compromised by parading for fire-fighting in rugby kit. The sergeant was quite nice about it, apart from putting me on a charge. He read out a series of lunatic orders, apparently composed by the Duke of Wellington, the chief of which was, 'On the sounding of the alarm the fire picket will run in all directions shouting "*fire*". If any Government property is seen to be blazing they will surround it and challenge all who approach.' There was also something about not engaging enemy aircraft unless actually ordered to do so.

The sergeant then looked at me as if I was something out of a drain. 'Man-who-paraded-in-rugby-kit,' he boomed. 'Man-who-paraded-in-rugby-kit – wait-for-it – to the rugby match – dismiss.' And I scampered off.

The match had been in progress for a quarter of an hour when a miracle occurred. Lieutenant Bird actually held a pass. Blinking short-sightedly he set off for the opposition line, with me outside him, and passed. Unfortunately, at that moment the camp fire-alarm sounded. Without faltering I swerved neatly off the field and ran to the guardroom bellowing *'fire'* at the top of my voice. Lieutenant Bird found me five minutes later and politely asked if they could have their ball back.

After that I seemed to be on fire picket rather a lot.

Rank used to be the great problem of Service sport. It was difficult for a private to skipper a team full of sergeants, when on Monday they would be telling him what a horrible little man he was and handing out punishments. That is assuming they paid any attention him in the first place. In my day sergeants paid no attention to anybody else on the field except another sergeant. There was also the problem of mixing after the game, and officers usually had tea elsewhere and kept to themselves in the evening. An old pal, Ted Hart, who used to play for Eastern Counties, swears that once in the war he was the only non-officer in a military team and they made him eat at a separate table.

I freely admit my somewhat jaundiced attitude is due to the fact that my unit side was in the hands of an unfortunate lieutenant nicknamed Pinocchio. He picked the side in descending order of rank, irrespective of ability, starting with the Major and then going downwards. There were only about five or six rankers in the side and after a time we became disenchanted and refused to play. Pinocchio retaliated by making every game a parade so we had to turn up, and we struck back by bleating like sheep every time we took to the field. Eventually the Major, a kindly

HARO

soul, suggested we ought to have a trial match to pick out the best. By scouring the unit and borrowing from miles around, it was just possible to raise 29 men and then unfortunately the Colonel agreed to make up numbers. I say unfortunately, because he made it plain early on that he resented being tackled by anyone of inferior rank, and since there were no brigadiers playing, that meant everyone. The result was that if he fell on the ball everyone stood around respectfully waiting for a more senior person to arrive and kick him off it. Pinocchio could not bring himself to do violence to his commanding officer and used to say 'Excuse me, sir,' before making a tenatative jab at the ball with his foot.

The same protection did not extend to more junior officers and one or two old scores were settled. A captain was the first victim, being felled from behind by a Rugby League player who had just returned from a field punishment centre. Nobody knows who jumped up and down on the adjutant but it was definitely not me who was ordered, by the hapless Pinocchio, to stop kneeling on his loins.

I feel the spirit of Pinocchio lives on in the current Army edict about names. But the practical implications are rather alarming. When half the side have to be called 'sir' how does anyone know who's being addressed? And what about those long military titles? It's not much use shouting 'Quick, outside you, acting company quartermaster sergeant Smethurst.' By the time you've spilled that mouthful he's been tackled. And what if you don't know a player's rank? Surely even the Army Sports Council don't suggest that players sew stripes on their sleeves or pips on their shoulders.

In the end I suspect the Army will deal with the difficulty in its own special manner. After all, they have been coping with impossible orders for hundreds of years. Like so many stupid edicts, the whole thing will be quietly ignored until it goes away.

5

What Did You Do to Ronald?

The Secretary,
Old Rottinghamians RFC
Power Station Lane,
Rottingham.

Dear Sir,

What have you done to my son?

Ronald left hom after a light lunch yesterday to play rugby with your club for the first time. Although I myself have never played rugby, I gave my blessing to the idea because Ronald is a shy, delicate lad who has never belonged to any clubs or sporting bodies except the local philatelic society, and we felt the experience would draw him out. I have read many speeches by leading officials of the Rugby Union and from these I gather that it is supposed to be a splendid game for developing a sound physique and a good character. In short, we hoped it would make a man of Ronald. When he left home he was sober, in his right mind and well dressed.

Imagine my feeling when a shambling, mumbling derelict was deposited outside our front door at midnight.

I was aroused from bed by a prolonged ringing of the front-door bell, and on opening the door I beheld my son leaning with his elbow on the bellpush while two dim figures could be discerned scurrying round the corner. At first I could not recognize Ronald. His mouth was severely contused and there was a mass of dried blood on his left ear. Someone had apparently rowelled his cheek with a set of nails. The end of his tie had been cut off. Worst of all, he reeked of stale beer fumes and was able to talk only in a mumble.

At the sight of me he burst into laughter and started to bawl some verse about the daughter of a character called O'Reilly, which contained words of such a disgusting nature that I was obliged to place my hand over his bruised and battered mouth to prevent his mother hearing them.

Ronald was removed to bed and undressed, being incapable of doing this himself. To my horror I then found his back was branded. Someone called 'Taffy' had written his name across Ronald's back with a red ball-point pen. The inscription would not wash out, despite the application of detergent, and I presume it will have to stay until it wears off.

Ronald was too ill to get up in the morning, but in the afternoon I questioned him about what had happened and was unable to gain any clear explanation, except that as it was the first proper match of the season there had been some sort of a celebration. His mother told me that there was a large lipstick stain on his collar. He could not account for this.

I can only hazard a guess at what went on. I demand, sir, an account of what happens at your club, otherwise I shall place a copy of this letter in the hands of the President of the Rugby Union and the Chief Constable.

Believe me, I am not a spoilsport. When younger I frequently indulged in good-humoured horseplay and bonhomie after an exhilarating hike, but this is too much.

Your faithfully,
R. Foster

OLD ROTTINGHAMIANS RFC

Dear Mr Foster,

It was jolly decent of you to write and I'm sorry you were so upset. Actually we were a bit worried ourselves. You see, the Rugby Union is trying to urge everyone to start up Colts' sides because so many youngsters are coming into the game, and we thought we ought to have one, and Ronald, of course, should have played in the Colts, but only three blokes turned up (I told the committee we could never do it, but they wouldn't listen). Well, the Extra B were seven short, so we put the Colts in the Extra B and I'm afraid they were playing some old enemies of ours who have a lot of old-stagers in the side (Welsh, you know) and the match was a little rough. Actually, Ronald hurt his ear during half-time when someone kicked the ball to him and he wasn't looking. As regards his cheek, I believe somebody trod on his face. Don't worry, we know who it was and will be looking for him next time we play them.

Well, being the first night of the season we had a little 'do' in the new pavilion and I'm afraid that during this Ronald put his foot through the plate-glass window at the front and broke it. I'm told this will cost about £500 to replace and we aren't insured so I'm wondering if you could see your way to do something about it?

While on the subject, we are still short of some £10,000 to pay for the pavilion and as you are obviously interested in sport I wondered if you thought of becoming a non-playing member of our club?

It costs only £10 and this entitles you to see every match for nothing and to use the bar whenever you want (officially we shut at ten-thirty, but you can usually get something up to midnight if you go in through the little door by the visitors' changing-room). We have a flourishing darts team, a football swindle and an annual sweep on the St Leger. Last year one of our players was reserve for a county trial match, so we hope that at last the old club is on the up-and-up.

I look forward to hearing from you.

Yours sincerely,
A. Brown, Secretary, Old Rotts RFC

PS We are starting Bingo sessions in the clubhouse every Thursday, beginning next week. Ladies welcome. Why not bring your wife?

6

Coarse Captaincy

During a game of rugby one player may be seen lagging behind the others, but nevertheless uttering hoarse cries of encouragement from a position thirty or forty yards behind the ball. This is the captain. It is a safe bet to say the standard of captaincy in the average club is as low as the standard of handling, which is to say a great deal.

Everyone recognizes a good captain. His team wins. As long as the side keeps on being victorious the man nominally at their head will be considered a fine skipper.

It is not so easy to spot a bad captain. One infallible way is to listen to what he shouts during a game. A good captain will either say something specific like 'Put it into touch' or will shut up. The bad captain delights in meaningless exhortations such as 'You're not getting stuck into them' or 'For heaven's sake do something, forwards!'

For some reason bad captains loathe any move that varies from the conventional. An attempt to make a deceptive drop out merely brings forth a snarl and a shout of 'Cut out the fancy stuff.' The only way to gain approval is to put your head down and charge the opposition at their thickest point. Then, after the carnage has settled with a gain of about six inches, the skipper will shout that

that was great, that was the sort of stuff we want, not fancy juggling (with a fierce look at the last offender).

Such skippers have a wonderful knack of getting on the wrong side of the referee. They achieve this by snorting heavily at every decision against their side, muttering 'Oh God' and glaring at the offending official. The only effect this has is to increase the number of decisions against the team, and if the referee has any sense he makes a mental note to warn all the other referees as well.

Another of their charming habits is to upset the biggest and toughest forward on the other side, shouting from a safe distance, 'Cut that out, you dirty bastard.' Then they keep well out of his way, leaving some innocent player to suffer retribution.

If any member of their own team complains about anything they tell him to shut up. But if they feel that injustice has been meted out to themselves they demand support from all fourteen.

I shall not easily forget playing for a side whose skipper was ordered off the field (and quite rightly too). He immediately turned to the rest of the team and demanded that they march off in support of him. Fortunately we had enough sense to refuse, whereupon he announced the whole side would be dropped next week for failing to obey captain's orders. Only the fact that he himself was expelled from the club the following Monday evening stopped him carrying out his threat.

Perhaps, though, men like that are preferable to the bundle-of-energy type who is determined to Transform the First Team. Such players rarely have any tactical knowledge, but believe that fitness conquers everything.

His side is plagued by a host of injuries caused in training, and the constant cross-country running reduces everyone's match speed to a steady jog-trot. However, the team do have the satisfaction of knowing that if they can ever get within reach of their less fit, but more skilled, opponents they will pulverize them.

Captains like this often have high-sounding theories about physical fitness. They know a little elementary biology and take pleasure in telling players that the slope of their shoulders affects the leverage in the scrum, or that their bowels are too long, or some such gibberish. As a cure for bad passing they recommend sexual abstinence not only during the game, but before it, after it, and even when you've given up rugby. I knew one captain who issued a diet sheet for the First XV, and would strike sandwiches from players' hands with a cry of 'Too much starch.'

Then there's the Whiz Kid. He does it all by exhortation and propaganda. Like the West London captain who stuck posters all over the clubhouse, urging everyone to greater efforts with slogans like:

IT ALL DEPENDS ON YOU

or

TACKLE! TACKLE! TACKLE!

He even wrote to every member of the team before a big game, urging them to maximum efficiency on the Saturday, but the letters didn't usually arrive until the Monday, when they had already lost heavily.

This captain was a great one for speeches, and he never lost an opportunity of addressing a team before a game. Unfortunately, his speech usually had the opposite effect to that intended.

'Listen lads,' he would shout, leaping on to a bench. 'This is a game we've simply got to win. We've got a few old scores to pay off against this lot. Remember what they did to Charlie Evans last season? Broke his leg in three places. And gave old Mike Flynn fourteen stitches in his head.

'Then there was poor Freddy Perch. Got five teeth knocked out in the return match. And Jack Smith was kicked unconscious. Are we taking this lying down?' At this point several weaker members of the side would turn pale and look around for a way of escape.

'Luckily,' the captain would remorselessly grind on, 'they've got the same team out as last year. Which means you've all got a chance to take revenge. In particular watch that big front-row forward with the shaven head. Whatever happens don't be frightened of him. He may weigh seventeen stone, but the bigger they are, the harder they fall . . .'

Having reduced his side to quivering apprehension, he would lead them on to the field crying, 'Okay, lads, let's go, let's get stuck into them right away.'

The club newsletter provided him with a splendid platform and the captain's notes filled it page by page to the exclusion of more interesting material. At the annual dinner he used to ramble on for half-an-hour so the chief guest (who had probably driven one hundred miles to be present) had to cut his speech to three minutes; at the annual meeting he went on for ever, unless physically restrained. There was nothing to be done about him, he could talk his way into everything, except victory.

Yet one must sympathize with a captain. It is a lonely task, made all the more difficult by the fact that sudden promotion can mean the end of old friendships. It's no use pretending people feel the same about their old pal when he drops them. Nor when he rebukes them for employing what used to be his favourite tactic, like deliberately collapsing the scrum.

The secret of successful leadership is a continual pose, the constant pretence of emotions you don't really feel, such as feigning anger that you're only two points up, when actually you're astonished not to be losing by twenty. For this reason, mournful men make the best leaders – they don't have to pretend. One of the most successful skippers I met was a whining pessimist who never had a good word for anybody.

'Don't get over-confident,' he would groan, as the full-back banged over the fiftieth point. A winger who scored in the corner after running seventy yards would be told he ought to have touched down between the posts. Once he got the score wrong, thought a conversion had been disallowed and came off the field abusing us for losing.

When someone explained we had in fact won, it made no difference. 'You needn't think that alters things,' he snarled. 'There's more to winning than just scoring more points than the other side.'

A Coarse captain faces special problems. One is that the side don't want a leader of men, they want someone who will make life easy for them. The first quality is skill at cancelling a game if the other side looks like being rough or the weather's bad and there is any possible excuse. I used to play under a man who was a genius at avoiding play. Many a time we left our burly opponents snarling in thwarted rage as we all trooped away to get drunk, our skipper having bluffed his opposite number into believing the pitch was unfit.

It's only when you lose someone like that you realize how lucky you have been. Once he could not play and we got a former First XV captain who spent ten minutes persuading a reluctant opposition to play on a frozen pitch, full of razor-sharp ridges. Despite shouts of 'Stop it, you fool,' he succeeded, and I still have the scars. Fortunately he was one of the first victims, being carried off with a plug of frozen mud in his ear.

Consider a Coarse captain's duties. By these I don't mean the normal responsibilities of captain, keeping an eye on the tactical situation, switching centres and that sort of thing. Generally the Coarse captain is spared most of those since any attempt to influence team play will only bring forth abuse. His real duties begin on Sunday morning, which he will probably spend making vain enquiries as to why half the side didn't turn up the day before. There will also probably be an unpleasant interview in the bar with the club chairman on the lines of 'This sort of thing gets the club a bad name' as if there was anything he could do about it.

On Monday comes the selection committee meeting. This will start with stern enquiries as to why the fifth team had only eight men. Having spent their venom, the rest of the committee cheerfully grab all the available players for themselves, working downwards from the first team, so that the Coarse skipper is left with eight men, two children, a cripple, a man who hasn't been seen for six weeks and several blanks which the team secretary promises to fill during the week (he hasn't any intention of doing anything of the sort).

Tuesday is training night. Left to himself, the Coarse captain would not dream of appearing, since he long ago reached the stage where training merely increases the danger of physical injury, strains, ruptures and so forth, but he feels he ought to set an example. This, however, is wasted, as not one member of the fifth team turns up.

Hints of impending disaster on the Saturday begin to arrive even at this early stage. The first rumours are heard ('By the way, Bert Smith says he's decided to take his bird out next Saturday . . . Jack Jones said he wasn't feeling very well . . .'). No one has the guts to drop out. They just spread a vague rumour and hope it reaches the captain before Saturday.

On Wednesday the Coarse captain returns home to find his wife has taken a phone message from the team secretary: Does he know of anyone who would like a game on Saturday? He moans to himself, 'It's happening all over again.'

On Thursday the captain receives a phone call from the club pyromaniac. They have been trying to get rid of this player for two years, ever since he danced naked on the tea tables at the Old Rottinghamians and later set the clubhouse on fire. Unfortunately he is deaf to all hints and gets a game whenever he wants by volunteering when they're desperate. Once again, the captain has no choice but to say he can play.

On Friday the Coarse captain goes to the pictures. He knows the phone will be ringing continually with bad news and he doesn't want to know it. Saturday is his day of horror, made bearable only by the knowledge that it will be over by 4.30.

If it is an away game, the Coarse captain heads for the assembly point (usually a pub) soon after midday. He is greeted by a stream of gibberish in the form of garbled messages. These run something like this: 'Jack told Jim to tell me to tell you that if he hasn't rung you by 12.30 he will go direct in Charlie's car, but if Charlie's car is still U/S then he will go with the rest of us, but in that case he will be a quarter of an hour late arriving.'

A desperate count of heads reveals nine players. The only two men in the side who can hold a pass have been taken away for the fourth team. But the club pyromaniac has turned up and is busy wrecking morale by telling younger players how the opposition are going to murder them.

On arrival at the opposition ground the first thing that greets the Coarse skipper is Charlie, with no sign of Jack ('But he distinctly left a message, old man, that he was going with you, not me'). A total stranger has joined the side, however, even though there is an uneasy suspicion that he thinks he is playing soccer for British Rail. One man has disappeared somewhere between the pub and the ground. The opponents kindly lend a half-witted youth to help make up numbers and play can begin.

Once the game is in progress, a Coarse captain's main job is simply an administrative one. First, he has to ration out his depleted forces, deciding which five of his twelve men shall go in the pack, which threequarter will have to play in the forwards, which forward shall be full-back and so forth. In this he will be hindered by the vice-captain.

The eternal vice-captain is the biggest pest in rugby. He persistently refuses to be elected skipper, because of the work involved, but considers it his duty to oppose every decision of the captain.

Having allocated his men (and ignored the vice-captain's grumbles) a Coarse captain has merely to hold himself in readiness to deal with any crisis, such as injuries or players leaving the field without permission. He need not waste his breath calling for greater effort, because once the game is set in motion it will roll on without any reference to him, no matter what he does.

His sole task is to act as spokesman for the side in any argument and to call for three cheers for the opponents at the end (or if the game has been a bad one, ostentatiously not to call for three cheers). The match itself is the least of all his worries.

These begin again as soon as the game is over. No sooner has he padded off to the showers than an informal inquest in the dressing-room, headed by the vice-captain, will blame the captain for defeat. There is not even any peace for the poor skipper in the showers, where, as he is sponging his armpits, a steam-covered figure alongside announces he won't be available for the rest of the season, and that he is thinking of trying to join another club as he is sick of being on the losing side all the time.

Unless there is a special crisis, such as telling the wife of an injured player that he has broken his leg, the Coarse captain may now have a drink. But not in peace. There is the beer kitty to organize, and this must be done swiftly before the non-social players slip away. And however ill he may feel, the Coarse captain must keep a smile painted on his face and try to make some sort of conversation with the opposition. Meanwhile his own men melt away behind him, leaving him with the usual unintelligible messages ('If I haven't rung Charlie by 4.30 next Friday, then he's got to ring you and tell you I can't play'), while the vice-captain leads away a little clique, all muttering.

In some ways, the Coarse captain doesn't mind the desertion. The other side are just as good company and much less of a worry. For a few minutes he imagines he might be left in peace. But wait . . . what is that in the corner? A sheet of flame bursts from the dressing-room doorway and a vacant laugh shows that the club pyromaniac is at his tricks again.

7

If I Was a Marrying Type

Dear Penelope,

I've got the most wonderful news for you – Rodney has asked me to marry him! It all happened as a result of the game at Twickenham last week. It didn't start very promisingly because Rodney's daddy wouldn't lend him the car and it took *ages* on the bus to Twickenham and when we went for a drink in the bar before the game someone pinched Rodney's Robin Hood hat and it took hours to get it back. They were all drunk and throwing it to each other.

I didn't really enjoy the game much, I couldn't see anything, and there was a great tall man in front of me and the only time I saw anything was when he bent down to pick up a cigarette he had dropped and I just caught a glimpse of two players punching each other while some more kicked another lying on the ground. Rodney said it reminded him of the desperate games they used to have at school, only of course he doesn't play now because he says you're too old at twenty.

Afterwards we went to the pub again and I've never *seen* such a crush of people. Everyone was singing by six o'clock. They sang 'If I Was a Marrying Type' and a simply disgusting one about a place called Mobile – I didn't understand half the words. About half past six

Rodney said we ought to move to the City Barge at Chiswick, because that was where the boys gathered, so off we went. It was terribly quaint there and I was enjoying myself madly when a positively *horrid* man in a filthy raincoat came up to me and said his name was Green and he was doing an article for a newspaper about the things spectators did after an international, and would we please do something exciting for him because up to now it had been like a vicarage tea-party. I didn't like the look of him one bit and I'm sure he wasn't a *real* journalist. He didn't look a bit like Rodney's cousin, and he gets pieces in *Varsity* at Cambridge. Also he smelt very strongly of rum, which made me feel sick. So I just ignored him and he sort of glowered and went off to the other bar. Later he came back and told Rodney he was a disgrace to the Extra B and unless someone started to do something he wouldn't have anything to write about.

About 8.30 Peter Williams gave us a lift to The Prospect of Whitby at Wapping and who should be there but this horrid man from the Press, only this time he smelt of beer as well as rum, and he was going about moaning that everyone was too well behaved, and then he belched right behind my ear (onions). The upshot of all this was that when we came to go home Peter's car wouldn't start and we were all wondering what to do when this horrid man came up and said would we like a lift in his car (he sort of *leered* at me as he said it). Well, I wasn't too keen, but Rodney jumped at the chance, so he took us back home, dropping Peter on the way.

When we got home he walked with us to the front door. I said 'Good night' very pointedly, but he didn't move and we were all arguing on the doorstep when Daddy came to the door to see what all the noise was about, and this horrid man took one look at Daddy and said: 'I know you, you were the dirtiest front-row forward that ever played for Melton Mowbray,' and Daddy simply *bellowed*: 'By gosh, I got sent off for punching you when we played Leicester Thursday.'

After that it was awful. Daddy and this man kept making foul jokes and upsetting beer all over each other, while Mummy simply *froze*. Eventually she went to bed, saying 'I hope you won't be long' to Daddy with one of those looks, but he didn't notice. Eventually I managed to manoeuvre Rodney into the back room and we were

HARO

sitting there with the light out when this horrid man came to the door and shouted: 'Be careful, my dear, I know his sort. He'll be trying to undo your blouse in a minute.' He and Daddy just roared. It was absolutely cruel of Daddy to laugh like that. Besides, Rodney's not that sort. Well, not quite (you know Rodney). It absolutely shattered the atmosphere and then they started singing that vile song I heard at Twickenham and Rodney decided to go. I went to bed absolutely *crushed*.

In the morning, when Mummy came down, she found a great stain on the dining-room carpet. Of course, Mummy was furious, especially when she found Daddy had been sick in the kitchen.

To make things worse, Daddy went off to meet this creature again at lunch-time at Kew Bridge and he and Mummy just sat and had rows all day. I felt absolutely wretched. Then Rodney came round in the evening and we sat in the back room and I burst into tears and said I felt so unhappy with Mummy and Daddy fighting all day, and Rodney was wonderful, he just said 'Don't worry' and stroked my hair. He's so *strong*. I hoped he would propose immediately but he didn't, so I managed another little weep and this time he popped the question.

Mummy was absolutely berserk with joy, but Daddy seemed to take it all coolly. I don't think he likes Rodney. All he said was: 'Which of the marrying types are you, sir? The scrum-half, I should think.' I don't understand what he meant. Later he went off to Kew Bridge and there was another scene.

I can't write any more because I've so much to do, sending letters and so on. I suppose I shall have to tell Jonathan. Or should I wait until after the French match? I mean, Jonathan's already bought tickets.

Love,
Fiona

8

Medicine Bag

One thing I've discovered over the years is that the quantity of kit carried by a player has nothing to do with the playing skill of its owner. In fact the amount of equipment used seems to get less as you go higher up the scale.

International players are liable to arrive in the dressing-room at Twickenham carrying an old carrier-bag, and casually ask, 'Can anybody lend me a pair of boots, please?' But ancient no-hopers, serving out their remaining days with the Extra C, will arrive at a match with great, elephantine boxes packed with every conceivable device for their protection and comfort.

They watch over these jealously, refusing to lend anything, not so much as a piece of cotton wool, making excuses like, 'I've only enough for myself. It's all right for you youngsters, but I'm liable to have a haemorrhage during the game.'

This vast load of baggage contains much more than the normal equipment of boots, shorts and so forth. Prominent among the additional kit will be a bottle, jar or vat of some magic potion. Older players cling to this sort of thing, swearing it will cure soreness, bruising and itching as well as rendering the user impervious to pain.

The magic potion may be rubbed on, rubbed in, spread

around the ears, squirted elsewhere, or even swallowed. Sometimes it is a well-known brand, but usually has an archaic title like 'Dr Turnip's Guaranteed Muscle Invigorator and Restorative', which the player boasts can only be obtained from a small shop in Limehouse or Stepney. In rare instances the potion may be home-made, in which case the inventor will enthusiastically offer to supply it all round the dressing-room. Do not accept, as upon applying it the skin may well turn black.

Other items in the older player's bag might include a roll of toilet paper (there's never any in the proper place); a Rugby Union handbook, which in emergencies will serve the same purpose as the toilet paper and can also be used for embarrassing the referee with awkward questions; vitamin pills; an optimistic contraceptive or two; the words of Eskimo Nell; a pyjama cord, which has a thousand uses from supporting shorts to stopping severe bleeding; and an old scrum-cap, irrespective of whether the player is a forward or not.

The reason for the last is the devastating moral effect of a scrum-cap worn by a threequarter. In most junior games the threequarters are delicate (that is why they are in the threequarters, not because they can run fast), and will curl up in fear at the sight of their opposite number wearing a scrum-cap, with its suggestion that the owner is really a tearaway second-row man filling in with the backs.

Even with a forward, a properly prepared scrum-cap has a great moral effect. No forward over thirty should ever set foot on the field without one. Before being used it should be carefully painted with blood. If you should write inside it 'Property of Bedford Football Club (RU)' and leave it before the game where the opposition will see it, so much the better.

The veteran's baggage may also include a tin of cough sweets; aspirins to kill post-match headaches or pre-match hangovers; and yards of elastic bandage. This is rarely used for its proper purpose, but more often for holding together boots which have split asunder or for wrapping round the hand with the adhesive side outwards – a sure method of ensuring you will never drop another pass. It is also useful for mending leaky car exhaust pipes.

Considering rugby is supposed to be a game for the fit and the strong, it's surprising how much kit consists of medical aids more suitable to a geriatric ward. I often wonder what people who don't know the game would say if they could peer into the average dressing-room and see men injecting themselves with insulin, strapping up vari-cose veins or even inserting suppositories. Others might be praying.

Then there are personal extras to suit individual tastes. My old pal Slasher Williams always carried a complete first-aid box when appearing against teams from the Coventry area. I knew another man who always packed his guitar, in the hope that after the match everyone would ask him to play. They never did, but they filled his guitar with beer one night instead. An Irishman used to bring his bagpipes even though he couldn't play them.

The same man wouldn't play without a religious locket around his neck to give protection against evil, bad luck, referees and wing-forwards. Unfortunately it provided an ideal handle for tackling him, and frequently the game would be interrupted by a cry of, 'Ref, some blaspheming bastard had torn off me St Simeon,' and play would be held up while we all searched in the mud.

If the locket wasn't found, play went on without Patrick, who crawled around on his hands and knees with his nose to the ground until he did find it, ignoring the complaints of players who kept tripping over him.

Alas, the modern habit of wearing brief trunks forbids the old custom of carrying a lot of essential kit on to the field of play itself, as one could do in the days of those long, baggy 'shorts' which finished just above the knee. No longer do player's pockets bulge with handkerchiefs and packets of lozenges.

Some pampered first-class sides provide all the kit a player needs. Many launder players' shirts for them. I always feel this takes some of the individuality out of rugby, because a man's potential can often be summed up by the condition of his kit.

My own experience has been that the man with the knife-edge crease in his shorts, and immaculate linen, is almost always an exhibitionist coward. The player to be careful of is the one stumbling about with an arm of his jersey tied on with a shoelace.

For a bachelor, looking after kit is an almost impossible task. If he doesn't wash it he can hardly move the following Saturday (I'm sure this is the real reason for the poor standard of running in most of the lower sides). On the other hand, any attempt to wash it at the laundromat blocks drains for miles around. Warning should also be taken from the experience of my old friend Taffy Owen, whose girl-friend washed his kit one Friday night in February, and hung it on the line to dry. When Taffy arrived to collect it in a hurry just before the game it had frozen solid, including his jock-strap, which resembled a Henry Moore sculpture. It was the only occasion on which I have seen a player arrive and stand his jersey in the corner of the dressing-room. An attempt to put on the jock-strap before it had thawed out resulted in the most terrible scream I have ever heard.

9

Thank you, Mr Sidewinder

The Annual General Meeting of the old Rottinghamians Rugby Union Football Club was held in the pavilion on May 31st. There were five members present when the meeting commenced at eight o'clock. This number later increased to thirty-six and then diminished to two.

The minutes of the previous AGM were read by the secretary. A motion proposed by Mr A. Jobling that the minutes were a travesty of the proceedings, and that the secretary had remembered it all wrong, was defeated.

The chairman then gave his report. It had been, he said, another year of steady progress for this grand old club. The playing record of won 7, lost 31, drawn 3, points for 96, against 433 might have been better (cries of 'No, you're kidding mate'). But there was more to rugby football than merely winning. Personally he did not go along with this modern emphasis on victory. The important thing was to play the game, play the gentleman and play the ball. Of course, victory was always possible by adopting such underhand methods as coaching and tactics. The French were adept at this, and we all knew what happened to them in 1940. He was proud to say they had boycotted the county coaching scheme.

He felt he could not conclude without a warning about the evil influences that were creeping into this grand old game of ours, helped by the sensationalism of the popular Press, although he was sorry to see that even the *Daily Telegraph* had now descended to criticizing that splendid body of men, the England selectors.

As an example of the evil influences, he quoted the fact that at least a third of the guests at the annual dinner failed to wear a dinner-jacket. Indeed, he had actually seen one of the younger players at a match not wearing his club tie. People were coming into the game who would never have been allowed in the old days.

Some were demanding more competition in rugby. Others wanted to make it more interesting for the spectator. Speaking for himself, he hoped he would never live to see the day when people enjoyed watching rugby. That sort of thing should be left to professionals. Personally he felt it was all somehow tied up with sex.

A motion that the chairman's report be adopted was passed by one vote to nil, the remainder of the members being in the bar when the vote was taken.

The hon. treasurer then spoke at some length. While everybody had a copy of the balance sheet, he advised them not to look at it, as they wouldn't understand it. The main point was that by writing up the fixed assets and writing down the floating assets, they had turned a profit into a loss.

A Member: Isn't that bad?

Hon. Treasurer: Not necessarily. Pounds and pence are meaningless symbols. A loss might well make more money for the club than a profit.

After several members confessed themselves baffled, the treasurer advised the meeting to pass the accounts as printed, as he had in any case no intention of changing them now, and he would try to explain it all afterwards.

The accounts were adopted by acclamation.

Arising out of the accounts, Mr Albert Sidewinder, a founder member of the club, asked whether money might not be saved on coaches if the first team would bicycle to away matches.

'I know times have changed since I was a wing-threequarter,' said Mr Sidewinder (cries of 'Yes, they've invented the aeroplane'). 'But I do know that when we used to play Beckenham some of us cycled over there and others actually walked, and we were none the worse for it, apart from feeling exhausted when we arrived.'

Mr Septimus Baffle then rose and said he was an even older member than Mr Sidewinder and it was not Beckenham they walked to but Bromley. Several players even ran there and back, sometimes tying their legs together to make it more difficult.

Personally he felt the modern player was too mollycoddled. Hot baths after the game had a weakening effect. In his day, after a match they threw buckets of river water over each other and apart from the occasional case of typhoid, they were none the worse for it.

It was all a result of abolishing flogging. He scourged himself twice a day and look at him now. The abolition of hanging had not helped. It would do some of these youngsters good to go down the mines.

At this point the chairman interrupted and thanked Mr Sidewinder and Mr Baffle for their interesting reminiscences, which older members had heard several times before, and declared the discussion of the accounts closed.

Mr Sidewinder: It would never have done for Bongo Paisley
(shouts of 'Pipe down, you old idiot' etc. etc.).

The election of officers then took place. All nominations were unopposed, with the exception of the third team captain, for which Mr J. Hardstaff and Mr F. Baker were both proposed. After a ballot, Mr Hardstaff was elected by seventeen votes to nine, with eight spoilt papers. Four members who attempted to vote twice were also disqualified.

After Mr Hardstaff's election, Mr Baker rose to address the meeting. On being told that he was out of order, and in any case there was no need to stand on his chair, Mr Baker commented that everyone knew the club was run by a clique. He had given the best years of his life to the club and this was what happened. As far as he was concerned they could stuff the third team and its new captain right up the drainpipes.

Mr Baker then adjourned to the car-park and blew his horn for ten minutes as a gesture of protest.

The chairman then announced any other business.

Mr P. Pettigrew said he knew he was speaking on behalf of most of the second team when he queried the methods of team selection. 'I scored two tries against the Old Bagfordians,' he declared, 'and instead of putting me up to the first team they dropped me to the thirds.'

The team secretary replied that he had some sympathy with Mr Pettigrew, but he had been dropped to the thirds because he had a car and it was an away game. He suggested that if Mr Pettigrew really wanted promotion he should sell his car.

Mr Pettigrew said he was flabbergasted and dumbfounded. This explanation accounted for a lot. They had better watch out or else (cries of 'Hear, hear').

After several members had complained that certain privileged people could get drinks after closing-time, the chairman declared the meeting closed. A vote of thanks to the chair failed for lack of a seconder.

10

Why the Whistle Went

At the end of a rugby match a morose person may sometimes be observed sitting alone at the bar and scribbling on a bit of paper. It is the referee and he is only waiting until they condescend to pay his expenses before going home. Meanwhile he is filling in time by sketching out a report on why he sent someone off.

Yet start swapping stories with a rugby player and two-thirds will be about the referee. Abused, maligned, ignored (and occasionally appreciated) he remains firmly woven into the very fabric of the game, more than in any other sport. Certainly when I asked for stories about referees in *The Sunday Times* they arrived like a deluge, and it is significant that many of them came from referees themselves.

A charming yarn from a former Irish international, J. I. Brennan, now of Devizes, described the time he refereed a match in County Down. To his surprise there weren't any corner flags, so he broke off branches from a nearby hedge and stuck them in. Six months later he returned to officiate in another game, and the branches were still there – but by now they had taken root and were sprouting a fine crop of green leaves.

Considering the abuse referees have to endure, a surprising number of letters featured him as the hero with an all-seeing eye. Vivian Davies, of Swansea, told of a match in which the official was Gwynne Walters, famous Welsh referee of the fifties and sixties. As a young man, Walters was in charge of a West Wales Cup semi-final which erupted into a pitched battle between the packs and ended with a player stretched out cold. Walters looked at him and shouted across to the touch-judge, 'When this player comes to, tell him he's been sent off!'

Somewhat similar was the incident recounted by Derek Kemp of Avon RFC, in which a Welsh referee stood over a man as he lay groaning on the ground and warned him, 'Now look here, Mr Ifor Jones, if I see anyone kick you again, then OFF YOU GO!'

But referees don't always show such perspicacity. George Neilson, of Edinburgh, recalled playing at Penarth for Royal High on the morning of an international and being the victim of a foul blow which knocked out several teeth. The referee 'rebuked' the offender by saying, 'That was disgraceful. If this wasn't a friendly I'd send you off.'

Referees are often accused of being blind, but Gil Thomas, of Combe Down, Bath, who is in his seventies, once played in a match controlled by a referee who was totally deaf and relied on lip-reading to find out what players were saying. Unfortunately Gil had a habit of chewing gum on field. After an unjust penalty was awarded against him he was chewing extra hard in irritation when the referee marched up and jabbed a finger into his chest. 'Any more language like that,' he barked, 'and I will send you off the field!'

Back to the thirties, when J. V. Billeter, of Harrow, was playing for a Wasps XV against Harrow. The referee, a fat little man, kept getting in the way of a huge Wasps flanker called McCabe. Five times the big man ran round the scrum and slap into the referee; the sixth time he picked him up and threw him aside with a cry of 'Get out of the — way.' The referee landed in a puddle and lost his whistle. Play continued while he crawled round looking for it and calling for help. In the end five players were sent off and stood on the touchline booing the unhappy referee. And the giant McCabe? He became a priest.

Hector Taylor of Gunnersbury Crescent, West London, described playing in Argentina in 1929 for Buenos Aires (then an English club) against an Argentinian side. When the British referee awarded a penalty kick to the Englishmen, the Argentine skipper asked why. 'Because they are my friends,' replied the referee with a deadpan expression. The Argentinians calmly accepted the explanation and play went on.

Many referees produce novel rebukes in time of trouble. S. R. Vernon, of Vale of Lune, remembered a referee who shouted, 'If we have another outburst like that I shall abandon the game, and what's more the bar will remain closed because I have the keys.' This had an instant effect. Bill Rudderham, of Chiswick, recalled a referee who sent off an elderly offender with the gentle words, 'I think fifty-five minutes is quite enough at your age, old chap.' R. H. Bishop wrote of a very posh forward who gave a complicated argument justifying his offence in highly cultured tones and was given an equally academic reply, 'You do realize we can continue this game quite well without you, don't you?' But perhaps the most polite threat was recalled by a friend who said that when she was playing ladies' hockey at Blackheath, one of the umpires told a player, 'If you do that again, Mavis, I shall ask you to go and put the kettle on for tea.' Try saying *that* to the Pontypool front-row . . .

Sometimes, of course, the referee is on a hiding to nothing. Like one described by R. Head, of Norton St Philip, Bath, who warned a persistent offender in a junior game that he would be sent off next time he committed a foul. He received the reply, 'In that case I might as well go now – I wasn't too keen on playing today, anyway.'

Denis Morris, who played for Blackheath and Leicester in the twenties and thirties, wrote that he was once rebuked by a rather decrepit referee for an offence he didn't commit. When he protested the referee said, 'Well, if it wasn't you, it was mighty like you, and if it happens again I'll send you off.'

Among the referees who wrote in was Jim Crowe, a former first-class official, from Leigh-on-Sea. He remembered a referee who rather pompously told two bickering teams, 'There is only one referee on the field today.' To which came the immediate reply from an anguished forward, 'Then for God's sake give him the whistle!' Somewhat similar was the experience of Brian O'Hanlon, of London Irish, playing a game in a junior side controlled by a rather poor Army referee, who announced in his best parade-ground manner, 'Now look here all of you, there are too many referees on this field.'

'Yes,' agreed Barney Murphy, an Irish forward, 'and you're by no means the —ing best!'

However, the letter I liked best and which was well out of the usual run of yarns about violence and thuggery, came from K. E. Ellis, of Halifax, who reported hearing the following dialogue on the field:

Referee: What is your name, Smith?

Player: What do you mean, what is my name? You know me.

Referee: You are a disgrace to the game! Get off the field!

Player (with amazed look of disblief): You can't send me off. I'm your brother-in-law!

There is a glorious Pinter-like quality about that conversation, with both parties talking yet totally failing to communicate. But then, perhaps only a writer of Pinter's quality could do justice to the sort of situation referees often find themselves in.

Touch-judges are a different kettle of fish to referees since, except in representative games, they are not neutrals, but members of the clubs concerned. I remember a team in Leicestershire just after World War II whose touch-judge was a raving psychopath. At his best he would merely award all line-outs to his own side and shout encouragement as the ball was thrown in; at his worst he would charge on the field and beat opponents with his flagstick. I suspect most clubs have someone like that tucked away in their history, although I doubt if many would have a touch-judge as weird as one I met, who patrolled the touchline in an electric chair, and once steered it on field and into the back of a ruck. He was an ex-captain recovering from serious injury, and after his incursion on to the field someone disconnected his batteries and left him gibbering helplessly.

Plenty of that type of touch-judge get 'sent off' by the referee, of course. Graeme Pratt, chairman of Crowborough, had his flag officially taken away just because he loudly agreed with a woman spectator who criticized the referee in his hearing. Graeme is now a referee himself.

Jeffrey Knight, of Coalville, Leicestershire, wrote in about the time he was playing on the wing against Syston, and his opposite number, aggrieved at a tackle, kicked him up the backside. Not to be outdone, the Coalville number eight, a veteran player in his twentieth season, did the same to the Syston winger. This so enraged the Syston touch-judge that he rushed on to the pitch and began to assault the number eight. The referee immediately went over, shouting 'Off! Off!' and pointing to the dressing-room, and the number eight slunk away, only to find the referee didn't mean him, he meant the Syston touch-judge.

A North London player told of a formidable woman touch-judge, divorced mother of a young fourth team player, who insisted on running the line to keep an eye on her son. She was rather biased in his favour and constantly abused the other side. They had to dispense with her services after her son had made a run down the wing, and was threatened by the opposing full-back. As he went to make the tackle, she thrust her flagstick savagely into the full-back's groin – and he went down gasping in pain while her son sped past. During the following week the club chairman called upon her at home to explain that the club would reluctantly have to ask her not to officiate again. What transpired at the meeting will never be known as shortly afterwards they both eloped and lived together happily.

Eddie Pugh, of Thurrock RFC, described what must surely have been the most arrogant touch-judge of all time. At an away game in Hampshire, as Eddie stood behind the posts for the first penalty, the local touch-judge calmly said, 'As home official I am senior to you, so I'll decide if the ball goes over.' Eddie also told of a referee who invented a completely new signal for touch-judges. 'I'll decide who puts the ball in,' he said, after overruling Eddie a couple of times. 'If you have any doubts, raise both hands in the air!' He then made a gesture as if surrendering. 'I have not been able to use this unique signal,' wrote Eddie, 'as he has never been asked to referee us again.'

Diana Thompson, of Wootton Bassett, daughter of a former chairman of my old club, Ealing, wrote in to remind me of Ealing's famous touch-judge, Jack Prisk. Jack, a legendary character who had served in both World Wars, ran the line until well into his seventies, but had to give up when a scrum wheeled suddenly and collapsed on top of him, breaking his leg.

And another unusual angle from Peter Piper, of Black-heath, who recalled that when he was touch-judge his main duty was to save injured players from a trigger-happy doctor with the team, who always wanted to perform an instant tracheotomy with his penknife. After a narrow shave when a player choked on an apple in the coach and was only saved from the knife when someone thumped him on the back successfully, Peter had standing instructions from several players that if they were hurt he should rush on and scoop them away before the medico could get at them.

11

Hélas! Quel Slam!

*(Scotland won their first Grand Slam
since 1925 when they beat France 21–12
at Murrayfield in 1984.)*

M'sieur,

You ask me how I feel and I am telling you I have
desecrated myself. My cistern of sorrow is overflowing. It
is the worst day since the EEC butter subsidy failed to
arrive. I have not felt so desolated since that English lorry
broke through my road block.

Yet this match he is so exciting. I am hardly able to
speak. To start we are in despair when Dods kick a
penalty, but then came the try by Gallion. What artistry!
M'sieur, he swerve round the side of the scrum like *un taxi
parisien* trying to run down an elderly pedestrian in the
rue de l'Opéra *à l'heure de pointe*.

Then there is that terrible time with the balls sailing
over the bars and we are level 12–12. There is a fateful
line-out, my heart is in my nostrils, and behold! – Calder is
over. *Quel catastrophe!* We cannot come back now.

It is only twenty-four hours since I am arriving in
Edinburgh for *le* Grand Slam with my friend Jean-
Baptiste and I tell you the city she is nice but the food they
are not so good, eh? Last night at our hotel we have the
grand vin d'honneur and Jean-Baptiste is bet 500 francs he
cannot finish a bottle of whisky, but *quel courage* he drinks it
in one, and later his *visage* turn *un peu* black and he is
carried away.

We drink many toasts to our heroes, to Rives and Gallion and to the martyred Garuet, dismissed against Ireland by the perfidious Norling when an Irishman thrust his eye against the noble Garuet's thumb, and we remember that this time the *arbitre* is also from the land of the Gauls.

But this morning we march proudly up Princes Street with our cardboard cockerels, our national emblem, and I say to *un agent de police*, 'Have you ever seen so many people waving their cocks in the street?' and he say *ma foi*, no, not since the Festival when anything can happen.

So we march to Murrayfield. At *la Gare* Haymarket we have great hunger. At home in Cherbourg I eat at our *siège social*, Le Café du Théâtre, before *le* match, so we enter a bar and call, 'Allo, mister, some *moules marinières*, a few *huîtres, peut-être des crudités* and a bottle of Muscadet *bien froid, hein*?' and the man reply, 'You've got a hope, Jimmy,' and gives us the national dish, which is pieces of *gendarme*'s leg with *haricots carbonisés*, but *sacré bleu*, it tastes like the exhaust of an old Citröen pick-up truck.

Beside us is an *Écossais* in a skirt with a paint brush over his *organes privés* and I think he is a little tipsy as he knocks over my beer and I shout, '*Zut alors!* What a *dommage!*' and he replied, 'And up you too, Jacques,' and I embrace him because he calls me by my name instead of Jimmy.

I ask him about this man Rutherford, and he tells me Rutherford is a right shocker, and so is Laidlaw, and he is shocked if they don't shock the shocking French, and I am interested in his use of the idiomatic speech as the *Écossaises* have a reputation for purity of the language, but *hélas*, our friend suddenly cries 'Shock me' and goes outside where he is *trés malade, une grand explosion sur le trottoir*.

At Murrayfield we unfurl our banner which say *ALLEZ FRANCE* in *majuscules*. *Hélas*, we do not have our old banner *DEMISSION AUX SELECTIONNEURS* which we wave in *le Parc des Princes* last year. We spit on the committee as they arrive, but they spit back even harder (*sans doute* coached by the good Jean-Pierre Rives) and then the *gardes mobiles* tear up our banner and say they will do the same to us if we do not stop spitting on the selectors. So I spit on the *gardes mobiles* instead, but I am better now except for a slight limp.

And so *le* match *commence. M'sieur.* You know the rest . . .

12
Dinner is Served

Human beings have an incredible capacity for self-torture on social occasions, otherwise the amateur dramatic movement would have collapsed years ago. Rugby clubs are far from immune to this little failing, and much prone to a form of self-induced suffering called the Annual Dinner.

The vilest form this takes is the Prestige Dinner or Posh Nosh, an event much-beloved of London clubs. This is held in the West End, adding £3 in fares to the £20 members will be paying for their tickets, a good deal of which goes towards subsidizing a swollen guest-list, most of whom never wanted to come in the first place.

The menu is moderately extensive, but the portions would just about satisfy a starving gnat. The wine list looks like a builder's quotation for repairing Buckingham Palace. All wine arrives at the table lukewarm, irrespective of colour. So does the food. It will be served by swarthy little men who do not speak a word of English and who usually bring the wrong bottle.

Beer may also be served, at a king's ransom for each short pint of lukewarm foam. Change (if any) will arrive on a plate with a strong implication it should be returned to the man who dispensed the foam.

Drinks after the meal are, with fiendish timing, served

in the middle of a speech. The amount of noise and disturbance caused by this, and the desperate attempts of thirsty guests to order more, is increased by the waiter's habit of taking money and vanishing with the change. At one dinner, near Piccadilly Circus, I gave the waiter £20 for a £10 bottle of wine and he promptly disappeared, not only from the restaurant, but apparently from the district, since no further trace of him could be discovered, although we had six people searching every back alley for miles around.

Speaking at such functions is an ordeal. One is introduced by a bellowing idiot in a red coat calling himself the toast-master, and the opening remark is probably drowned by an ear-splitting screech from the microphone. Subsequent remarks are made with the white-gloved hand of the insane toast-master moving the microphone up and down in front of your face. Meanwhile, out front a riot appears to be going on as guests argue with waiters bringing the wrong drinks and disappearing with the change.

But eventually the proceedings drag to their conclusion and those guests who have not missed the last train can carry on drinking glasses of foam or whisky at prices which seem to increase as the hour gets later. This period gives senior members of the club a chance to bemoan the fact that younger players won't come to functions of this sort.

And as the last guest (usually a vice-president who has been sick over his evening suit) is helped into the lift, all is silence except for the sound of the staff counting money, a process that will probably take them all night.

A more common dinner, however, is the Suburban Gin Palace Feast. This has the advantage that the price is more reasonable than in the West End, and the robbery less violent. Among disadvantages are platoons of stout, middle-aged waitresses who hover round the room during the early speeches, imposing a rigid censorship. Service of drinks after the meal ceases entirely, and the food is variable, and often made more unpalatable by the waitress's habit of thrusting her armpit into your face while serving it.

It's funny, but these dinners seem to have a peculiar effect on visiting speakers. Having travelled out into the backwoods, they become obsessed with the idea that it is their duty to educate the peasants. As the peasants don't feel like being educated, at least not at the annual dinner, the speech turns into a sort of slanging match between the speaker and the club members.

Veins stand out on the speaker's forehead and he starts off in a manner that would make a Pharisee turn green with envy. 'Gentlemen,' he thunders, 'I would like to begin by saying that one of the things that distinguishes a rugger man from another is that he has a code. Tonight the behaviour of some of you has not conformed to that code.' (A piece of cucumber flies past his ear.) 'I do not approve of trying to interfere with waitresses while they are serving soup for a start. Neither could I approve of the remarks of the previous speaker when he made irresponsible criticism of the amount of money the Rugby Union spends on banquets.

'Gentlemen . . . gentlemen . . . would you shut up at the back there . . . gentlemen . . . as I was saying earlier to your splendid President, Mr Carpenter' (cries of 'His name's Wright') '. . . as I was saying to Mr Knight . . . we have to return to the old standards. Did someone ask what standards? I would say the old standards did not include throwing a piece of cucumber at the chief speaker!'

And so the battle continues for some ten minutes until the speaker gives up his educational efforts and sits down to scattered applause and a few boos from the far corner, while brushing the odd piece of cucumber from his coat.

Apart from speeches like the above (which are sometimes delivered by the nicest people), another hazard of the Gin Palace Dinner is the professional comedian who may be employed to entertain. Fortunately, they usually have to give up their act halfway through when the noise is so great that no one can hear a word, or indeed wants to.

The Club Supper is more informal and usually held in the pavilion. The food is not much worse than in the previous two examples, and the supply of drink a good deal better and cheaper, although the finer table wines may be lacking, and if served at all, will contain a generous percentage of cork and cigarette ash.

The object of any speaker at these functions is simply to provide a target for bread-rolls and sugar cubes, so that all he is expected to do is to stand up, remain vertical for three or four minutes, and sit down without losing his temper. If, during that period, he can recite every obscene word in the English language, so much the better. He will, in any case, probably find someone has stolen his speech notes if he left them on the table. Once, someone *burned* mine and had the cheek to return the ashes in a saucer with a note, 'Your speech was hot stuff.'

Occasionally, a professional stripper appears after the coffee. This eagerly awaited and much whispered-about entertainment is normally an embarrassment, as the lady in question turns out to look rather like the captain's mother. Her performance is not improved by people pretending to be sick at her most tantalizing movements, or trying to throw sugar lumps at her navel.

Unhappy though the above examples may be, they pale before the dreaded dinner-dance, now becoming more and more popular.

The whole trouble with a dinner-dance is that owing to the presence of women it is not a dinner, and owing to the presence of rugby players it is not a dance. The result is an evening unrelieved even by dirty jokes or snide references to the first-team threequarters. The main interest comes later when domestic squabbles break out between wives and husbands, and one realizes why some players are always quite keen to come out training.

To make things worse, the seeds are sown of future infidelities. All too often, the result of holding a rugby club dinner-dance is that next season two legs of an eternal triangle will be found packing together in the second row, with subsequent dire results on the playing record.

You have been warned.

13

Insult to Injuries

There are two attitudes to injury among rugby players. The first-class men are worried, not so much by the pain involved, to which they appear to be impervious, but by the fear of losing their place. Most of them have studied the subject and are familiar with the effects and symptoms of injuries not only on themselves but on other players. The more unscrupulous will not hesitate to play on an opponent's known physical weakness such as a recently healed shoulder or leg. When Tommy Gray, the Scottish international, was playing for Northampton just after World War II there was a rumour that because of a war injury to his foot he could only jink to the right. Tommy used to encourage the rumour because in emergencies he could go to the left and leave opponents floundering.

But as one descends the rugby scale, so attitudes change. The Coarse player's main concern, as he lies groaning on the grass, is that the injury won't be serious enough to stop him playing. He is like a wounded soldier who asks, 'Is it a Blighty one?' Few pleasures in life equal that of standing smoking on the touchline with a harmless sprain and watching all hell being knocked out of your side, knowing that now they can't pick you for the sevens.

It may seem surprising, but there are more injuries in

Coarse rugby than in the proper variety. Surprising indeed when one considers the average speed of a Coarse player is about half that of a first-class man, and also that there is very little tackling in Coarse rugby. Indeed, I have seen a whole game played without one recognizable tackle. All moves broke down simply through bad passing or the knack a Coarse player has of falling down when no one is within miles.

Despite this, Coarse players are subject to injuries which do not affect others. To start with, many are hurt while running away.

I remember standing in the next shower to a young lad whose back was a mass of scrapes and bruises. I gazed in admiration and asked if he had been kicked when falling on the ball.

'No,' he said, 'I was trying to get out of the way of a forward rush and I tripped and fell on my face and they all trampled over me.'

Age is another cause of injury in the lower echelons, and I write as one who has seen a man leave the field with the excuse, 'My varicose vein is throbbing.' Nobody thought it unusual.

This particular player was about fifty and suffered from a terrible crop of middle-aged troubles. After one scrum broke up he was left standing by himself in the middle of the field, bent over at right angles. It was one of the most extraordinary sights I have ever seen.

We gathered round in awe and the referee asked what was the matter.

'Lumbago,' he replied firmly.

We led him gently away, still bent double. He had to be taken home kneeling on the floor of someone's car.

He also had a nasty habit of suddenly turning blue and gasping for breath with a terrible rattling noise which sounded like an old car starting up. Everybody thought he was going to drop dead and stood back in fright. If he had the ball they wouldn't dare to lay a finger on him, and occasionally he took advantage of this to wheeze and rattle his way over for a score. The opposition were always very annoyed when that happened and made comments like, 'Don't ask *us* to give you the kiss of life, mate.'

Sheer physical unfitness is the cause of many Coarse rugby casualties. I used to play with a forty-year-old threequarter in the third team who had once been brilliant but who could by then manage to play only in short bursts. In the first half he made a run, collapsed about five yards from the line and then walked off the field and lay down. The referee ran over and asked what the trouble was.

'Nothing,' he said. 'Just leave me here till half-time, will you?'

At half-time he slunk over to the pavilion and had a glass of rum, and in the second half made another run. This time he scored. Without waiting for the kick, he walked straight off the field and into the showers. We won, which just goes to show he was worth his place.

Coarse rugby can be responsible for some strange injuries. I have seen a man injured by the touch-judge's umbrella (which was open at the time, shielding him from the rain) and I knew a chap who was nearly drowned in the Grand Union Canal because my side, who were winning, deliberately kicked the ball into the water. While trying to reach it with a long stick he fell in, after which it was discovered that he could not swim, a fact of which he informed us somewhat excitedly as he came up for the third time.

In the end our full-back rescued him, but had the intelligence to leave the ball in the canal.

Mental ailments are as common as physical ones. There used to be a team in Hertfordshire with a forward of such frenzied disposition he had to take drugs during a game to relax him. Everyone was warned beforehand, so when the wretched youth began to foam at the mouth and leap on some opponent, everyone merely stood around saying 'There, there,' and fetched his tablets. Apart from this unfortunate habit he was quite a good forward.

Considering the nature of rugby, the casual attitude towards first-aid seems remarkable. Even at first-class level medical facilities may be limited to an appeal for a doctor. Many clubs rely on the St John Ambulance Brigade, a splendid body of men who unfortunately appear to have been recruited from the ranks of polio victims. It is a fifty-fifty chance that by the time they have collected all their gear and reached the victim, he will have recovered. They tend to be obsessed by stretchers, and whatever the nature of the injury will scour the district for one before lurching on the field with it.

They have only two methods of treatment – applying a splint or pouring water over the victim. This is at least an improvement on referees, who have only one cure for all ailments – to bend the sufferer up and down. Usually all three methods are tried, just for luck. The St John men are even slower at getting off the field than at getting on it, and play frequently continues around them. A friend claims he was injured by the unique method of running into an ambulance man and cutting his head on an overcoat button.

The worst people to play against are medical students. They love to practise diagnosis, preferably something as serious as possible, and they never agree. While the player lies groaning he hears a conversation like this:

'Don't move him whatever you do, or he'll never walk again . . .'

'I think his spine's gone, Rodney. There's no reaction at all when I kick it . . .'

'Nonsense, his spine's all right. It's his pelvis. Look at the way he's lying. It's broken in two places.'

'Well, you may be right. I haven't done the pelvis yet.'

Fortunately the diagnoses are invariably wrong. I even heard a first-year dental student diagnose someone as dead, whereupon he sat up and was sick.

Strangely enough, first-aid facilities at hospital grounds are always worse than anywhere else. It takes hours to find a stretcher, and when one is discovered it is mouldy with age so when you lift it up the patient falls straight through the bottom and adds a bruised back to his other injuries. The last time I played a hospital they couldn't even cover a small cut because the cricket team had taken all the elastic bandage to bind up their bats.

In general, it can be stated without contradiction that at a hospital ground, the only person capable of administering first-aid will be the steward's wife. Despite the frozen welcome which casualty departments hand out to hurt rugby players (they seem to regard rugby injuries as tantamount to self-inflicted wounds) it may be safer to insist on going to hospital. In this connection, have no truck with the team sex maniac who always 'knows some of the nurses at St Swithin's' and who invariably recommends one to some broken-down cottage hospital without X-ray facilities.

Only once have I seen expert diagnosis by a hospital rugby team. While playing their third side I left the field with a suspected broken rib and a fourth-year student came over to have a look at me.

I told him it ought to be X-rayed.

'Nonsense,' he said. 'I've got a certain method of diagnosis.'

Whereupon he simply punched me violently on both sides of the chest simultaneously.

I sank down on a bench in pain, but conscious.

'Ah,' he said wisely, 'you can't have broken it. If you had, you'd never have been able to withstand that.'

The dreadful thing was that he was right. I feel he deserved to pass his finals.

14

Selectors in Session

It is a wet Monday evening. Six men are seated round a table in a deserted rugby pavilion. They are the club chairman, a stout, red-faced man of about fifty, the team secretary, who looks rather like an extremely worried rat, and four team captains whose ages range according to their status, so that the First XV captain is a blond giant of twenty-four while the skipper of the fourth team is even older and fatter than the chairman. The selection committee are in session.

Chairman (taking a gulp of beer): Well, gentlemen, I think we're agreed that last week's result was very, very disappointing. I don't think the Old Rottinghamians have ever beaten us by 45–nil before.
(There is a general murmur of agreement, mostly in the form of curses and oaths.)
Chairman: The question is, gentlemen, what do we do? We have another tough game against the Vipers next week.
First XV Captain: We've just got to have another scrum-half. That new chap was hopeless. And he said he used to be a Welsh schoolboy international.
Team Secretary: He was a hockey international.
First XV Captain: Well, I wish you'd told me. The centres

never saw the ball. I think we should push up Jackson
from the 'A'.

Second-Team Captain: That's out, for a start.

Chairman: What's the matter? Hasn't he paid his sub?

Team Secretary: No. But, then, only five of the first team
have.

Chairman: This is absolutely disgusting. It would never
have happened before the war. If you didn't pay
you were out straight away. Suspend the lot of 'em, I
say.

(He bangs his fist violently on the table and upsets beer
all over his trousers.)

Team Secretary (after order has been restored): If you
suspend every man who has not paid his subscription
that will include the club skipper, his entire threequarter line and half of this committee.

First XV Captain: Never mind about that now. It's just a
minor administrative detail, that's all. I want to know
why we can't play Jackson against Vipers.

Second-Team Captain: If you must know, he's having an
affair with the wife of the Vipers' captain.

(After a moment's shattered silence there is a babble of
noise as the committee ask for more details.)

Third-Team Captain: Not that blonde who came to the
dance? Ghaaaaah . . . she had smashing legs.

(He drools into his beer.)

Fourth-Team Captain: I thought he was going out with
Angela Roberts. He certainly gets around.

Team Secretary: It all started at the dance. I saw them
sneaking across the car-park, hand in hand . . .

Chairman: Gentlemen, please. This is not a women's
institute. This is a serious matter. I've said it before and
I say it again, there's too much sex in rugby. In the old
days you didn't go to a rugby club dance to go sneaking
across car-parks hand in hand with some popsie. You
went there to shout and drink. This rot is going right
through the game. Before the war no decent player ever

dreamed of seeing his girl on a Saturday night. Now they won't even stop for a pint before sloping off after some female. No wonder the country's morals are up the creek.

(He pauses for breath and beer.)

Third-Team Captain: I say, there's a lot of funny bits at the bottom of my stout.

Fourth-Team Captain: You want to write and complain, they give you a free trip round the brewery.

Third-Team Captain: Honest? I'll preserve the bottle as proof.

(He goes behind the bar.)

Chairman: This bounder Jackson must go. Expel him, throw him out. Warn him off. Write to the Rugby Union. Glub.

(He drinks deeply.)

Third-Team Captain: All this stout has got bits in it. Do you think we could claim a new crate?

Fourth-Team Captain: What you want to do is to drink half of each bottle and then return them all.

(He goes to the bar to help.)

First-Team Captain: Well, we'll just have to switch Clark from the wing to scrum-half and promote Higgins from the 'A'.

Second-Team Captain: That's out too. Higgins has a car. If you take him we'll have to go by coach.

Chairman: Before the war we never had cars and coaches. Went everywhere by train. I remember Alf Edwards filling his plus-fours with bottles of light ale on the Brighton line. We drank the lot by Haywards Heath. Threw a bottle out of the window and hit a porter. All good clean fun. None of this sex business in those days, gentlemen. At least, not on Saturday night.

Third-Team Captain: By the way, only nine of my men turned up last week.

Fourth-Team Captain: That's funny. I had seventeen.

Team Secretary: Yes, I know, I'm sorry about that. My

young son peed on some of the postcards and I couldn't
remember who was supposed to play where. Anyway, it
doesn't matter, you'd have lost just the same, only you
wouldn't have lost by so much. Try and be philosophi-
cal, old boy.

Chairman: Gentlemen, let us pursue the task in hand. All
right, just a half.

First-Team Captain: Suppose we switch Brown from centre
to stand-off, bring Robson out of the pack into the
centre, switch Robinson from full-back to wing-
forward, promote one of the 'A' wing-forwards to act as
first-team hooker and use old Charlie as scrum-half?
He's just the build.

(There is a long way silence.)

Second-Team Captain: Say that again.

First-Team Captain: It's simple. You switch Brown from
the centre . . .

Chairman (hastily): No, no, I'm sure there's a simpler way
out.

Team Secretary: Of course, you can tell the Vipers that
we won't play Jackson if they'll agree to drop their
skipper.

First-Team Captain: You can't tell a side to drop their
skipper.

Second-Team Captain: The alternative doesn't bear thinking about. Suppose they met in a maul? It'd be murder.

Third-Team Captain: Personally, I think Jackson should be
operated on. He even made a pass at my wife. No
woman's safe while he's around.

Chairman: I wish I could place this Jackson chap. New,
isn't he?

Team Secretary: He's a little thin-faced dark chap. Got a big
scar on his cheek.

Chairman: Talks with a Yorkshire accent?

Team Secretary: Yes.

Chairman: And drives an old Renault?

Team Secretary: Yes, he does.

Chairman: Good God, I think he's taking my daughter out tonight!
  (The meeting adjourns in disorder as the chairman leaves for home hurriedly.)

15

Cowardy Custard

Despite the fact rugby is supposed to be a game for the fit and strong in body and spirit, most rugby teams have their quota of yellow-bellies, or full-blooded cowards. Whole teams may be composed of loud-mouthed cravens, shouting for someone else to 'tackle, man, tackle' as they pant round a suburban field.

Yellow-bellies even infiltrate the highest levels, and the average international side usually has one or even two, although they are frequently skillful enough to disguise the fact. The superb footwork of many a top-class stand-off has been developed not as an attacking weapon, but because the player is scared stiff of being caught by the wing-forwards.

Standards of courage, of course, are higher at the international level and what might be quite acceptable for the Extra First won't do for Wales. Outside of the senior teams, falling on the ball isn't compulsory. If you can do it, so much the better, but if you prefer to fly-kick you won't lose your place. After all, the skipper is probably doing the same sort of thing, although this won't stop him bellowing, 'Fall, damn you, fall,' on every possible occasion.

The philosophy of rugby is rather peculiar in its attitude to cowardice, which is considered the ultimate sin, while inefficiency, which is much more dangerous, is considered excusable. The worst thing that can be said of a player is that he lacks guts, but I have seen far more matches lost by players who lacked intelligence than by men who lacked guts.

It is regarded as unforgivable to shirk a tackle, but quite all right to run wildly at the runner and fall over when he sidesteps. Similarly, any man who refuses to fall on the ball is sub-human, but someone who falls on the wretched thing, refuses to get off it and gives away a penalty which loses the match suffers little, if any, criticism.

Fortunately, cowards have a natural affinity for each other on the rugby field. They know. Speaking as a five-star, ocean-going coward myself, it was always a great relief to find the person opposite was not one of the bulldog breed. You can usually tell in the first tackle – it's the look in his eyes as you bore into him, the shifty, hunted glance that says, 'Let's all be pals, we don't want any rough stuff, do we?' Sometimes he will communicate more directly, smiling or muttering an ingratiating remark.

Forward cowards tend to do a lot of shouting, piling in the back of the rucks with great oaths, but they take care not to be too near the ball, where all the scrapping is going on.

Full-back cowards have a wonderful sense of timing which allows them always to arrive a fraction of a second too late if someone is following up a loose ball, unless he is a coward as well. If another yellow-belly is chasing the ball, the results can be a little bizarre, with both players timing it superbly so that neither of them reach it, and then approaching in slow motion.

Stand-off is sheer hell for a coward, especially if he has a funk of a scrum-half who gets rid of the ball to save himself punishment, no matter how closely the fly-half is marked. For years I played scrum-half to a man who actually used to shout 'Don't pass' as he stared with horror at the advancing wing-forwards. Not that I paid any attention –

as far as I was concerned it was him or me, and fear lent fantastic length to my passes.

Perhaps it was only justice that eventually they moved me to stand-off (the threequarters hadn't received the ball all season), where I developed a masterly technique for missing the scrum-half's pass and making it look his fault. It took some doing, but by a clever change of pace and a body swerve, followed by a despairing groan, I could guarantee to be nowhere near the ball, no matter how good the pass was.

I think the most astonishing act of fear I ever saw was perpetrated by a player called Galloping Jenkins, so named because of his jerky nervous run, and his habit of tossing back his long hair.

Although he had the guts of a particularly feeble sheep, Jenkins could run, and in one game broke right away down the wing. About twenty yards from the line he was challenged by the full-back, a front-row forward who had been seconded to the position for reasons which will be understood by anyone who has played that class of rugby. Thinking he could pass this leaden-footed oaf with ease, Jenkins jerked away on a prancing side-step and stuck out his arm wildly to hand off. His outstretched fingers went straight into the full-back's eyes and he staggered back shouting, 'I'll get yer, yer dirty bleeder.'

This threat was reinforced by a spectator who called out cheerfully, 'He means it too. He fractured someone's skull last season.'

With a squawk of fear, Galloping Jenkins ignored the line and turned round and ran back towards half-way, pursued by the angry full-back. On reaching half-way he kindly offered the ball to anyone who would take it, but observing the snarling man-mountain moving up the field no one would accept. Eventually, Jenkins retreated to his own twenty-five, where fortunately he had the good sense to put the ball into touch.

This, however, made no difference to his pursuer, who

continued to chase him off the pitch and down the path. We were playing in a local park at the time, and the full-back returned saying he had 'chased the bastard as far as the Great West Road, but then he escaped in the traffic.'

16
It's All Off, Penelope

My Dear Penlope,

Rodney and I have broken off the engagement!

I've got to tell someone or *burst*. It all happened last night. Rodney rang up just before lunch yesterday, and what do you think? He was actually playing rugby! Apparently some old school friend asked him if he would make up numbers for a team called the Vipers or the Boa-Constrictors or something (anyway, it was a snake) and although Rodney always says he's too old at twenty he said yes, he'd play, and he asked me if I'd watch the match and then stay on for the club Christmas Dance in the evening.

I didn't really want to watch the game (I never understood it when they all put their heads together in a huddle), but I did so want to go to the dance, so I said yes and I slipped into a lovely hot bath and used up all those gorgeous cubes Jonathan bought me and put on my new dress, the one Rodney likes so much, although I think it's a bit low at the front.

Rodney came about two and drove me to the ground in his Daddy's new Jag (the one the firm bought him) and then I had the shock of my life! My dear, the ground was just a *morass*, with a cinder-tip at one side and a power station the other. My stockings got all spattered in a puddle and I asked Rodney to carry me, but he never was very strong and had to hand me to a huge fat man who carried me in a rather familiar fashion I thought.

Then we had to wait an hour until everyone turned up and even then the other side had only ten men, but Rodney said it was all to the good, they would have a nice easy game of it.

Well, when we got out to the pitch the first thing that happened was that my stiletto heel sank into the ground and I was absolutely rooted to the spot. I just stood there bawling for aid and no one paid any attention at all, they just played on as if I didn't exist.

After about half an hour I think Rodney must have offended somebody, because there was a lot of shouting and arguing as they lined up under the crossbar and then he was moved from the centre of the field out to the wing because they blamed him for letting a try go by or something.

A few minutes later the ball came to Rodney and he began to run towards the line, which was only a few yards away, when he was challenged by an enormous bloated individual from the other side. He was at least as old as Daddy and *huge*. He sort of shambled towards Rodney with his arms brushing the floor and snarling like an animal, and Rodney simply stopped, shrank back and then threw the ball vertically into the air.

Apparently you shouldn't do this, because there was a positive *howl* of execration. I thought they were going to lynch Rodney from the goalposts. The captain was beastly, and used absolutely foul language, including *that* word (you know, the one Daddy uses when he misses the ball at golf).

After that Rodney just slunk up and down the field muttering to himself. I felt a bit sorry for him, but I must say his performance didn't fit in with what he used to tell us about playing in the first XV at Oakham.

Eventually the moronic game ended (I think these Vipers people lost, because their captain refused to give three cheers for the other side, he said they were a dirty lot) and we went back to the pavilion. I was just warming my hands round a cup of tea when a stark-naked man padded right across the room on his way to the shower. He was all covered in hair, like an ape, and had pimples all over him. It was disgusting.

After tea I asked Rodney where the dance was and he said didn't I know, it was here? I was simply flabbergasted, because it was just a brick barn with a concrete floor and a bar fifty feet long down one side. Well, it was too late to do anything about it, so I hung around while they kept passing revolting jugs of beer from hand to hand. I didn't have a chance to talk to Rodney because for some reason or other he had to collect all the money for the beer and none of them would pay. But a little Welsh chap named Taffy Owen was very nice to me and bought me several gins. Then about eight Taffy said the band had arrived and showed me a man fixing up a record-player at one end.

I have never been to a dance like it. The first thing that happened was that just as they got going a great gush of dirty water shot out of the showers and flooded the floor. I had to stand on a chair. They said someone had washed his kit in the showers and blocked the drains and one or two people swept the water away with brooms, but it still left a ghastly deposit on the floor.

Then things went from bad to worse. I was seized by the nasty fat man who had assaulted Rodney (he reeked of rum) and he dragged me round and round in some sort of reel that went on for ever and then in the middle of it all one man fell down and they all pounced on him and tore off his trousers and poured beer all over him.

I looked round desperately for Rodney and found him

propped up against the bar and I said firmly: 'I want to go home, Rodney.' He gave me a terribly profound look, as if he had some great secret to impart, and lurched from the room. I think he went to be ill.

I just stood there helpless when this Welshman came up and told me how he used to be a schoolboy international and how he would have played for Wales but he injured his leg saving fifteen men in a colliery explosion and he said ever such nice things to me and how he liked my dress, etc. etc.

All this time there was no sign of Rodney and Taffy went to look for him and came back and said he was feeling so sick that someone had driven him home. I nearly burst into tears. I thought of ringing up Mummy and asking her to pick me up (I knew Daddy wouldn't) when Taffy offered me a lift. Of course I grabbed at the chance, honestly within a few minutes I wondered if I was going to come out of it *alive*.

As soon as we got into the car he drove straight into middle of a deserted wood. It took me hours to persuade him to move from there. After that he drove home by an extraordinary route which consisted entirely of dark alleys. It was two before we got to the house and even then I had to *fight* my way free and in the morning Mummy asked me what were those marks round my neck and Daddy burst out laughing.

At lunch-time I rang Rodney and demanded an apology. Do you know what he said? He wanted *me* to apologize, because apparently he hadn't been driven home at all, he was just being ill outside, and when he got back to the dance he found I'd gone home with Taffy. He actually accused me of deserting him.

Well! I realized immediately that would never work out and sent his ring back at once and he called round later to return the Robin Hood hat I gave him last Christmas. Daddy had the cheek to congratulate him. Sometimes I *hate* Daddy.

I shall have to finish now, as I can see Taffy's car arriving. Will write soon.

Love,
Fiona

PS I wouldn't mention about Taffy to Jonathan, if you don't mind.

17

Forecast Stormy

A Coarse rugby player's views on bad weather are rather different from those of better players. First-class clubs make every effort to play; hot-air blowers, braziers, even flame-throwers are used to thaw the pitch. Armies of volunteers clear away snow. Both teams turn up for the game and jump up and down cursing their luck. But the sight of a frozen pitch, or a lake of water where half-way used to be, gladdens the heart of Coarse players and rejuvenates ageing limbs. It means they are to be spared the ghastly torture which normally ruins Saturday. The only problem is how to gain a thirst for the evening's social duties.

It is, of course, important not to reveal too much pleasure at a cancellation. I knew a man who jumped in the air and shouted, 'Thank God for that. Now I can ejoy Saturday afternoon,' when the captain announced the game was off, and the skipper, who was a rather keen type, wouldn't have him in the side again. Ideally, the Coarse player will mutter how disappointed he is and what a pity it's not even fit to train as he was really feeling in the mood for a good, tough match.

Sometimes play starts even when conditions are really too bad to play properly. Here the Coarse player comes into his own. After all, if the ground is so hard nobody dares tackle, not even the good players, that puts the Coarse player on a level with everybody else. Ditto if it's so wet that everyone is reduced to walking pace and no one can hold a pass.

Perhaps that's why, when I asked for bad-weather stories from readers, I got so many. Some extraordinary events were recounted, such as the story of what happened when Old Rishworthians of Halifax were due to play away against Sheffield Polytechnic. P. Simmis, who sent me the tale, says a prop named Braithwaite arranged to make his own way to the ground as he was attending a wedding that morning. He hadn't arrived at kick-off, but that hardly mattered as, after five minutes, the match was abandoned due to a blizzard.

'We returned to the changing-rooms and were getting dressed when out of the blizzard, across the field, loomed Braithwaite, resplendent in top hat and tails but covered from head to foot in snow. He rushed into the changing-room saying, "Thank God I'm not too late," tore off his clothes and proceeded to put his kit on. He was just smearing his body in Vaseline when he was brought to his senses by the sight of the team rolling about in tears of laughter. His language when told what had happened cannot be repeated . . .'

It's difficult to beat that, but some correspondents nearly succeeded. St Helens RFC, Lancashire, sent me a press cutting about their third team game with Fylde, played in dense fog. St Helens were delighted when Carl Atherton plunged over for a try, only to find that in the fog he had lost his sense of direction and mistaken the touch-line for the goal line. They lost 13–4. And A. F. S. Fairfull, of North Petherton, Somerset, recounted that he once scored a try in fog so thick he had to lie holding the ball while the referee searched for him.

David Howdle, of Pontefract, Yorkshire, wrote of a match between Harrogate Georgians and Hessle some years ago, played on a pitch covered with two inches of water, on top of which was a thin layer of ice. To make it worse there was a storm of freezing sleet, but the referee, a stern senior police officer, refused to abandon play. Eventually the Harrogate right winger, who had not seen the ball since play began, asked the referee if he intended to abandon the match. On being told, 'No', he thanked the referee for his services, shook him warmly by the hand, said 'Good afternoon' politely, and sprinted to the changing-room.

In those days, incidentally, Hessle had a coffin standing in the visitors' dressing-room, fitted with hooks like a wardrobe, for the referee to hang his clothes in. Unfortunately, the significance was lost on the martinet who officiated that day.

Not bad weather, but definitely an unusual interruption of play, was described by W. M. Jarvis, of Ham Common, London. Playing for K.C.S. Wimbledon against Whitgift on a foggy day in 1940, he looked up to see a German bomber appear over the pitch. It sprayed the field with machine-gun bullets and then vanished into the mist.

Bad weather started Bernard Dembo, of Maidenhead, on a lifetime career as a referee. He was dragged off the touchline to officiate in his wellingtons when fog delayed a referee's arrival and he liked it so much that he continued for ten years.

A story of disaster came from V. J. Skinner, of Riyadh, Saudi Arabia, about Solihull Veterans XV's tour to Bangkok and Pataya, Thailand, one Easter. Their first match was cancelled because the groundsman forgot to water the pitch and it was rock hard; they travelled to Pataya to find their next opponents, a Forces team, had had to sail away due to bad weather closing in. So they travelled 20,000 miles for no rugby at all – the Coarse player's dream tour.

Jeff Knight, of Coalville RFC, mentioned what must have been the most sadistic referee of all time. When the pitch was covered in ice for the annual Boxing Day match with Loughborough, he announced that the game would start, and 'We'll play rugby until someone gets injured and then we'll play touch rugby . . .'

But Gerry Davis, of Ilford, told the most bizarre story. It happened when Old Easthameians were due to play an obscure side from the Essex backwoods in the sixties. It had been snowing all week, but the Fourth XV waited until Friday night, when it became obvious the pitch was unplayable and Gerry, as captain, notified the fixture secretary, assuming he would tell the opposition.

At two o'clock on the Saturday afternoon he received a frantic phone call from one of his players, who had been out with his skis on Wanstead Flats.

'Through the snowstorm,' wrote Gerry, 'he had made out the unmistakeable shapes and noise of a rugby side, and gliding his way into their midst, discovered that the fourth team opposition had arrived and the Fixture Secretary had Failed Again.'

Gerry went over and spoke to the visiting captain, who refused to accept any apology. His lads were there and they wanted to play.

'I won't bore you with the details of picking a team up, getting dressing-rooms open and finding a referee,' Gerry continued, 'but we eventually kicked off at half past four in a none-too-pleasant atmosphere. I seem to recall we put thirty points through them and the only highlight of the game was when our full-back threw a snowball at the opposing scrum-half, but it hit the referee . . .'

18

A Mob on the Run

My old rugby club's annual Boxing Day pantomime, entitled A President's XV v. The Rest, and featuring an all-star cast of drunks and layabouts, will in future be held on their own ground, and the subsequent beer-swilling match will be in the new pavilion.

The news that the club has at last a home of its own will cause a sigh of relief among licensed victuallers throughout the entire district. During their years in the wilderness, playing on parks and recreation grounds, the club had led a sad, nomadic existence. How we envied those teams who had a long and happy association with one public house. But such good relations depend on having a landlord who is a wise bird and who on Saturday nights will provide a sound-proof, bullet-proof room next to the gents' toilet and let the lads get on with it.

Towards the end we ran through five headquarters in three seasons. The first lasted only seventeen minutes. It was a flashy, 1930-style place oozing chromium and waiters in little white jackets. Our first gathering was in the saloon bar one Saturday lunch-time to wait for the coach, and within a quarter of an hour the scrum-half had knocked over a table full of drinks; the captain had trodden on the landlord's dog; and the full-back had made an improper suggestion to the landlord's wife. The place was crammed with rugger players and their bags and the customers were pressed against the walls, defending their wives and their dogs.

The landlord said very quietly and sinisterly to the club secretary: 'Get that mob out of here before I call the police.'

One of our front-row forwards was a policeman, so he said: 'It's all right, my man, I am the police,' but the landlord merely replied: 'You won't be much longer when I've finished,' and picked up the phone.

Our policeman headed the rush to the door because he had feigned sickness to miss duty that afternoon and did not want his superintendent to know.

The next move was to a little corner pub near the park where we played and the landlord was glad to have us because he could make money from the teas. We lasted there some time until one Saturday our visitors insisted on playing darts, against our advice. The game got rather out of hand and ended with a dart striking the landlord in the back of the neck. Anyone would have thought it had been an Indian arrow, the way he carried on. I think he objected to the fact that the thrower claimed the landlord's neck counted as a double.

A further move followed, this time to a place with an upstairs room. We thought we were safe there, at least, but unfortunately the noise of the singing could be heard below. About eight o'clock one Saturday a red-faced customer burst into the room and shouted: 'How dare you insult my wife?'

Apparently his spouse was upset by the words of some of the songs (and not surprisingly). Before we could apologize he seized one of our smallest players by the lapels and hissed in his face: 'I'm going to make an example of you. Just step outside.'

Like most of the team our man was an arrant coward, but I must say he handled the situation beautifully.

'Of course I'll fight you, if you want me to,' he said

calmly. 'But I think it only fair to warn you that I am a judo Black Belt.'

I have never seen anyone's attitude change so quickly. The insulted husband assumed a feeble grin and slunk from the room muttering: 'No offence intended, I'm sure.'

However, this was but a temporary respite. One Saturday some fool in the team ran a competition to choose the

ugliest woman in the bar, and actually announced the name of the winner. He departed in a crash of breaking glass as her outraged husband leaped across the floor, and shortly afterwards the club secretary was seen sadly carrying our shove-ha'penny board to yet another public house.

This proved to be the best of the lot, and we stayed there a whole season, but we simply had to move because the beer was so bad. Eventually our oldest opponents told us there would be no fixtures next season unless we provided better beer.

This led to the final move. It proved a ghastly error. The hotel chosen was another big suburban place, but we went there because the landlord, who knew nothing about rugby players, said he would be pleased to have us. He even tried to persuade us to come.

'Your little group,' he said innocently, 'can have the billiards-room on Saturday nights. You can sing as much as you like. The last people to use it were the Bach Choir and they never disturbed us.'

Poor fool.

The billards-room was connected with the bar downstairs by a lift on which drinks were sent up. A whistle and speaking-tube were provided to attract the attention of the landlord. Nothing could have been more calculated to cause the final tragedy.

Our 'little group' duly appeared at six o'clock on Saturday, licking their chops thirstily, and the first move was to have ten jugs of beer sent up in the lift.

By nine the lift ropes were almost red-hot with constant use. The scene in the billiards-room beggared description. It was if W. C. Fields had played an exhibition match with Frankenstein. Snooker balls littered the floor. Two players were beating each other over the head with cues. Another was lying full length on the table, a cigarette in his mouth scorching the cloth, while he tried to pot a ball. The Extra B were stuffing snooker balls down someone's back.

At this point the club lunatic whistled down the shaft for more drink. When the landlord put his face inside the bottom of the shaft to ask for the order he simply poured a jug of beer down.

Hardened though we were, there was a moment's

horrific pause when we realized what he had done (apart from wasting the beer). We did not have long to wait. Within seconds the landlord, dripping wet, burst into the room, to be met by a billiard cue, hurled like a spear, which stuck quivering in the wall by his head.

At the annual meeting the figure of £300 was included in the accounts for 'sundry expenses in connection with club headquarters'. Nobody queried it.

19

Handling Heresies

Considering rugby is supposed to be a handling game, it's astonishing the number of players, at all levels, who are quite unable either to give or take a pass. It's only comparatively recently that anyone has ever worried about this, ever since the French started beating us by cheating, i.e. using forwards to run with the ball.

Not so long ago most forwards weren't supposed to know how to pass, and if they had to transfer the ball, they weren't expected to use the normal threequarter's pass, but a special one of their own, in which the arms were only used from the elbows. This was based on the theory that no respectable English forward would ever want to pass more than three feet, and if he did he should be damned well ashamed of himself. Forwards who threw long passes were equated with players who left the clubhouse early on Saturday nights to meet women.

I talk about this attitude to handling as if it was something in the past but there are still plenty of clubs where it holds good; where the forwards solemnly shuffle down the field at training, painfully handling the ball to each other from close-range, while the backs train separately, as if they were going to play some totally different game.

Why the whole basis of rugby should be its most

neglected aspect I don't know. Perhaps because of the English amateur tradition, that it's not good form to be too proficient at anything. Chaps who dance along the touchline balancing the ball on the end of their index finger have an unpleasant whiff of professionalism about them. Players who juggle desperately with the simplest of passes before knocking the ball forward three yards couldn't possibly be anything but amateur.

The schools must share some of the blame for handling standards. Frequently hours are wasted teaching boys a series of insane regulations such as passing off the correct foot, swerving the body and keeping the arms rigid (although they often forget the most important thing of all, which is to watch the man you're passing to). All this produces a peculiarly English form of pass, The Public School Swoosh, in which the passer is concentrating so much on the perfect action that he runs straight into an opponent while trying to remember not to bend his arms.

The Swoosh is seen much less frequently these days, thanks to improved coaching. But there are other types of pass which merit attention.

Probably the most frequently-used pass is the Helicopter. This is seen when a fourth team forward receives the ball ten yards from his opponents' line, with no one to beat. Does he stick his head down grimly, and with a snort of defiance head for the line? Or does he dance and swerve his way there, leaving would-be tacklers clutching the empty air?

No, he doesn't. What he does do is emit a ghastly shout of horror, stare wildly about him, and then throw the ball vertically into the air. It's no use saying that is exaggerated, if anything it's an understatement. It happens nearly every time.

Various theories may be put forward to account for this astonishing behaviour. It is not necessarily cowardice. The player is not afraid of any opponent, he is afraid of the ball.

This could be caused by intensive conditioning. Perhaps the unhappy player remembers when he was rebuked for running with the ball, and told a forward's job was to put his head down and shove. Or maybe years in the Extra B have sapped his self-confidence. After all, people aren't put in the fourth team because of their strength, sagacity, speed and scrummaging power. You're there because either you aren't fit for anything else, or else you have offended the club authorities in some way.

The second most common type of pass is The White Feather, an act of sheer fright by a terrified player. Signs of its approach start long before it is made, since the man with the ball will be seen running sideways, or even backwards, never taking his eyes from the potential tacklers.

When some fifteen yards from the nearest opponent, the player (still staring straight ahead) will take the ball in one hand and hurl it backwards over his shoulder somewhere in the vague direction of his own full-back. Without waiting to see the results of this, he will then fall over.

This pass is by no means restricted to the lower grades of rugby, and is even seen in first-class clubs who are playing stern opposition. Even internationals are guilty, but they usually manage to make it look like a cleverly-planned tactical move gone wrong, rather than an act of self-preservation.

The Gay Cavalier has been responsible for more lost games than any other factor. Its maker is inevitably a centre-threequarter, usually blond, who shatters the defence with a stunning break, flees for the line with his hair streaming behind him like a great mane, carefully draws the full-back and then hurls the ball with unerring accuracy two feet above the head of the unmarked winger, usually with such a force it goes deep into the crowd.

On one occasion in London, I actually saw a centre-threequarter pass direct into a No. 93 bus which was coming along an adjacent road. I may say that the conductor's return was considerably more accurate than the original pass.

One interesting aspect of The Gay Cavalier is that the passer has no sense of guilt whatever, and walks back to the centre of the pitch, tossing his head and smiling, stopping only to say to the winger, 'Bad luck old chap, but we all miss them now and then.'

If this should happen, resist any temptation to throw the ball at his face as he will have no idea he has done anything wrong.

Various positions on the field have their own type of pass.

Scrum-halves are prone to The Whirlitzer, the inevitable result of trying to pretend that you really do have a long pass, it just needs time to get there. The passer usually makes a tremendous fuss about delivering the ball, arching his back and flinging himself into puddles with gay abandon.

The ball is sent at an angle of 45 degrees upwards and hangs agonizingly at the top of its parabola before descending somewhere near the unfortunate stand-off, who is by now shaking hands with a particularly large wing-forward on the other side.

A variation of this is Casualty Ward, where the scrum-half runs with his head down in a tiny semi-circle, waits until the stand-off is surrounded and then squirts the ball to him from under his armpit.

Front-row forwards are prone to a particular pass of their own, The Presentation. Upon deciding to pass, a spasm crosses the face of the player, who then takes the ball carefully in both hands, rotates the upper half of his body carefully, and solemnly hands the ball, like a silver cup, to someone two feet away. For some reason which I can never fathom, he always finds it necessary to stop running for this.

Usually the best passing in a team will be by the

full-back. Getting rid of the ball for him is often the only way of avoiding a hideous death or serious injury. Most full-backs are capable of passing under incredible difficulties, using only the power of one finger, or even their teeth.

Finally there's a pass which doesn't exist – the Press Box Pass. The Press Box Pass exists only in the minds of sports reporters (including myself) and is usually described thus: 'England lost a great chance of going ahead when Smith broke through in the centre, only to ignore Robinson on his right and die with the ball near the line.'

The truth is that although Robinson was indeed on the right, he was thirty yards away, there was a high wind blowing, and three opponents were in the way of any pass. More important still, Smith was far too busy with his own problems, the chief of which was that he never thought he would break through, and having done so hadn't the faintest idea what to do next. Not to mention the fact that he knew unless he did something spectacular this was his last appearance for England.

A New Zealander once told me a novel theory. He said his coach worked on the rule that the receiver is always to blame for a pass going astray, since everybody should be alert to take the ball at all times. But I can't see the English accepting that. They prefer to stick to the old tradition that it doesn't matter whether a pass is accurate as long as you give it in the approved manner.

20

Beyond the Laws of Rugby

The Secretary,
Bagfordshire Society of Rugby Union Referees.

Dear Sir,

Please do not send us any more of your referees.

I must admit it was partly our own fault in asking your society to provide one. Normally, of course, our games are taken by a club member, but on this occasion he was ill. I may say he has refereed our games very well for fifteen years, moving with incredible swiftness for a man with one leg, and we shall be happy to stick to him in future, as he seems to understand our type of rugby better than your representative.

The team complain that your man upset them even before the game began by inspecting their boots, dress and persons. He not only declared that no fewer than five of our thirteen men had illegal studs in their boots, with the result they had to play in plimsolls, but he ordered our popular hooker, Paddy Flynn, to remove a signet ring from his finger. Mr Flynn is descended from a long line of Irish kings and the ring is a family heirloom. Perhaps I should have stated before that tradition says anyone causing the ring to be removed will die horribly.

Your referee complains that when the time for kick-off

arrived only ten players were on the ground, and his efforts to hurry up the rest were met with abuse. This may be so, but may I point out that he further delayed things by discovering that the ball was not inflated to a pressure of ten pounds per square inch at sea level, as I gather is required. There was further delay when he alleged the pitch was not marked out in accordance with the laws of the Rugby Union. I must admit that one end is distinctly narrower than the other, but this is compensated for by a bend in the half-way line. Anyway, we regard the interesting tapering shape of the pitch as a deterrent against indiscriminate touch-kicking.

The referee's action in playing forty minutes each way caused severe distress to several of our older players who are used to half an hour each half. But what disgusted our people most of all was his dastardly action in sending off Mr Flynn for persistently offending the laws. Mr Flynn assured me afterwards that he never knew standing on an opponent's foot in the line-out is classed as obstruction. I may also say it is our custom if a player is sent off to let him return if he apologizes properly. Mr Flynn proffered his normal apology at half-time and was rudely told to leave the field again.

When I interceded on Mr Flynn's behalf I was insulted to my face. Obviously your referee does not know that I had a county trial in 1956. Under the circumstances I do not blame Mr Flynn for hiding your referee's clothes, although I am sorry they were returned later in such a filthy condition.

Finally, there was absolutely no need to abandon the game just because the posts at one end sank into the waterlogged ground and eventually collapsed. Our normal procedure when this happens is to take all the kicks at one end and this has worked well enough for many years.

In future if our own referee is not available we shall do what we have done in the past, and that is to let the captain of each team referee one half of the game. Apart from a slight tendency to cause drawn matches, this always works perfectly well.

I remain,

Yours faithfully,

F. Fogg (Hon Secretary, Bagford Vipers)

PS At the conclusion of the game the referee had the audacity to demand £8 expenses from me. I was too dumbfounded to refuse, but my committee have now decided to ask for the money back, especially as we made a loss on the annual dinner again.

21

Danger: Lions and Cyclists on Pitch

One of the most important things a rugby player can learn is a knowledge of various hazards that are likely to affect him and his team before, during and after a match. I am not referring to playing obstacles, but to those unexpected incidents which add so much spice to the life of the rugby player.

Animals, of course, are a perpetual source of interruption and there is no need to dwell on the nuisance caused by dogs, sheep and cows. I have, however, had the interesting experience of being forced to move to another pitch because a goat had chewed through one of the goal posts.

Lions have been known to interrupt games in Africa. At least, so I am told by an old friend, who assures me that he refereed a match in which he was astonished when suddenly both teams, and the scattering of spectators, fled from the field, leaving him standing there blowing his whistle.

Eventually, cries of 'Simba! Simba!' from the African players, most of whom were up trees by now, drew his attention to the animal, which showed every inclination to go to sleep by the goalposts.

'I couldn't have that,' said the referee, 'so I pointed at him and blew a long blast.' The surprised lion shambled away – probably the first and last lion ever to be sent off a rugby field.

Normally it is the human element which causes most hazards. The most common of human-inspired hazards is undoubtedly Elderly Idiot Cycling across Pitch.

This danger exists primarily in public parks, although it can happen in enclosed grounds. It is most frequent when the playing area is bordered by allotments, in which case the offender will wobble wildly across the pitch with two sacks of seed potatoes and a garden rake slung over his back.

Never attempt to interfere with these people as upon being approached they inevitably fall off their bicycles, and this means the rider will probably spear his foot with a garden fork, and then you will never get him off the pitch. In addition he will shout and rave at all and sundry, bellowing insults like, 'Yer didn't oughter be allowed on 'ere, yer young hooligans, I'll report the lot of yer' etc., etc.

The only suggestion I can make for coping with an elderly idiot cycling across the pitch is to use him. Employ him as a shield and you will quickly find how difficult it is to be tackled when running behind a wobbling bicycle.

Banning of Game by Park-Keeper is another frequent hazard. The ban may be imposed because you didn't pay last week, because you're on the wrong pitch, because it's getting dark, because the pitch is unfit, or out of sheer cussedness.

The main point to remember is that nothing on earth will change a park-keeper's mind. They are a special breed of men, deaf to all reason and pleading, otherwise they wouldn't be park-keepers. Pointing out that the pitch is in perfect condition, offering money, threatening to complain, is worse than useless.

The only thing to do is ignore them completely. Play on as if nothing had happened, despite the fact that the wretched man is probably ringing a great bell at the side of the pitch. Eventually, he may walk on to the field of play and try to impound the ball, but it should not be too difficult to keep it away from him as park-keepers do a special type of walk, rather as if they have just had a vasectomy, which prevents travel at any speed.

Policemen Rushing on to the Field require different treatment. They will usually march on to complain about a parking offence, although in extreme cases I have known a policeman drive his motorcycle across the pitch. Their normal channel of approach is via the touch-judge, but they ignore his protestation 'You can't go on there.'

Under no circumstances attempt to continue the game or they will get out their notebook and ask the full-back his name just as the other side are about to score. Do not try to pretend that nobody knows anything about the car parked in the middle of the North Circular Road. The offender is somewhere around, desperately bluffing his way out of it. Make him confess and hand him over to justice without any mercy, adding sycophantic remarks like, 'You ought to be ashamed of yourself giving that nice policeman all that trouble.'

Any effort to shield the offender will merely result in examination of every car parked around the ground, and twenty summonses for such offences as having the rear number-plate obscured. The only person without a summons will be the chap who caused all the trouble in the first place.

NB: Never say to a policeman, 'Would you like a game, officer?'

A mishap experienced more than once is Sudden Mysterious Explosion of the Ball. This usually has nothing to do with its being forcibly kicked – it just goes off for no reason, probably age.

The traditional rule is the best here – if the first team's ball explodes, they are entitled to borrow one from the second team and so on, down the scale until the fifth stop playing (it is quite certain they won't have a spare ball).

A few seconds' consideration will show that this is a just

and reasonable procedure, because the fifth team will be
delighted at this opportunity to abandon the match and
get into the bath before everybody else.

And finally, a hazard that often faces a player after the
game, Failure of Hot-Water Boiler.

If that happens, never wash in cold water. It gives you
sores in winter weather. Simply leave the mud on like a
plaster. It holds the warmth, and you will be surprised
how comfortable you will feel for the rest of the evening. If
you are married, however, try to bath before going to bed.

22

Sixes and Sevens

When they picked me for the regimental seven-a-side team I applied to go on a Moral Leadership Course.

'What's all this about a Moral Leadership Course, Green?' demanded the CO when I was marched in. 'I should have thought Immoral Leadership was more in your line.'

The squadron clerk tittered sycophantically, the swine, while the sergeant-major said: 'Bejabbers and begorrah, 'tis the funniest man in the whole Army you be after being, sorr.' (He did not really use those exact words, but his Irish accent was so thick one can reproduce only the general sense.)

I set my jaw firmly and looked glassily at the CO's cap badge, which needed cleaning almost as badly as mine.

'I-am-tired-of-just-being-a-trooper-sir,' I intoned, in that peculiar voice one is supposed to use on occasions like this. 'I-want-to-be-a-leader-of-men. I-want-to-be-Someone. I-want-to-get-a-stripe-and . . .'

'Application rejected,' said the CO without looking up. 'You'll just have to play in the sevens, I'm afraid. And, Sergeant-Major, charge him with not shaving this morning. Bring in the next prisoner, please.'

I learned later that I was the fourth member of the

seven-a-side team to apply for the course that day.

I mention the story because it shows the lengths people will go to not to play in a seven-a-side tournament. I did avoid it, by the way, by volunteering for the brigade cross-country on the same day, and letting the orderly room decide. They promptly put me on guard.

To enjoy sevens one must be either dedicated or supremely fit. Most rugby players are neither, so the sevens loom as the only cloud on a perfect season. It would be fine if only one game was involved. But to win through to the final and to have to play perhaps four games in the space of five hours is nothing short of masochism.

As a spectacle, however, sevens are unequalled, especially if there is no danger of having to play, and one can spend a pleasant afternoon with a pint of beer in hand watching the cream of the country's youth run years off their lives.

Part of their charm is the rural atmosphere that surrounds a sevens tournament, rather like a mixture between a village cricket match and a church fête. An amateurish loudspeaker system booms forth misleading information in a distorted voice, preceded by an ear-splitting screech. Teams find themselves on the wrong pitches, playing the wrong opponents. Referees wander vaguely around, looking for their games.

The standard of refereeing is not always of the best. Once I heard a referee apologize to the losing captain after a game.

'I'm afraid I didn't really see that last try,' he beamed, short-sightedly. 'I only had my reading glasses on.'

Considering that he allowed a touch-down two feet from the line, one could appreciate that.

In the bar the fortunate teams who have been knocked out drink in thankfulness. Occasionally some still in the tournament do the same, with disastrous results. It is not unknown for a dazed player to mistake the result of a game, and drink himself into near-insensibility, only to discover too late that instead of losing, his side have won and he has another game to play.

Round the touchline the crowd contains an unusually high proportion of children and dogs since this is a family feast. Occasionally an infant may break from its mother and totter towards a line-out crying 'Daddy' piteously.

On the field astonishing things take place, especially when a team is losing heavily. If a player is on his knees it may be exhaustion, but more likely he is praying for the game to finish. The most dreaded thing is the long clear run of seventy-five yards with no excuse for not scoring. Often all that sustains a player on such a mission is the blessing of his opponents, who are flashing messages of goodwill, hoping he will score and knock them out of the tournament.

The only people who do not dread a run of this sort are a type which is the curse of a small tournament – first-class players turning out for their old club. Carefully attired in an old boys' jersey and England socks, they have a wonderful time making circles round the clod-hopping locals, who are reduced to complete immobility.

In the dressing-rooms every other team is a man short. Never bring your boots when watching a seven-a-side tournament. You will certainly be asked to play. It is safest to feign injury if between twenty and thirty. I know a man who always walks with a stick, just to make sure.

In contrast, the ground is sure to be haunted with at least one rugby prostitute, some player who feels cheated at being left out and who by happy coincidence just happens to have brought along his kit.

These players make themselves available to any side which is short. Like old One Run.

One Run came into our side after the winger had vanished just before the final, leaving a message that he had gone to Rangoon. He was an airline steward and he had to go on duty. From past experience he presumed we should never get this far.

One Run, a wizened, bald-headed little man of about forty, who had hovered hopefully round the dressing-room all afternoon, immediately volunteered his services. We asked the captain of our hosts about him and he said he played for their third team.

'He may be past his best,' he said, 'but he's always got One Run in him. Ten years ago he was a cracker.'

Well, we waited all the first half for the Run and it never came. At half-time we were 6–3 down and the captain approached our guest.

'Look, old man,' he said, 'I don't want to appear rude, but when are you going to do your One Run?'

One Run looked up panting. 'Just-huh-let-me-huh-get-my-breath ...' he gasped. 'I'll-make-it-huh-huh-you'll-see-huuuuuurrrrgggggggghhhh ...' (he coughed violently).

Well, a minute from no-side the score was the same, when One Run got the ball on our '25' and became positively galvanized. (I don't mean he became rust-proof, I mean he leapt into action.) I have never seen a man so transformed. Side-stepping like a Russian peasant being chased by wolves, he set off for the enemy line, leaving a trail of opponents flat on the ground, vainly clutching at his ankles.

On ... and on ... and on went One Run ... bounding over the half-way line ... jinking across the '25' ... spurting at full speed over the line ... and right over the dead-ball line until he slipped and collided with a car.

It was pathetic to see his face as he shambled back brokenly to the pavilion. Later he recovered sufficiently to have a drink in the bar, where a rather sharp-faced young man approached him.

'Are you the chap who did that marvellous run and then went over the dead-ball line?' he asked.

One Run glowed at the praise, and modestly admitted he was.

'Then I'm afraid I shall have to ask you for your name and address. You did fifty quids' worth of damage to my new Escort.'

23

Excuse Me . . .

Rugby is a game of excuses. This is not surprising when one considers what is required of the average player. The game has been designed, if played properly, to require immense stores of courage, physical endurance, instant decision even when threatened with three raging forwards, alertness, speed, self-control, the ability to assess what 29 other men on the field are doing in a split second and act accordingly, and the learning of some 400 paragraphs of laws, which are constantly being altered to make the game faster.

And if all that were not enough, a player is supposed to *smile* when hurled into the stand, grin when injured, shake hands with the man who kicked him, cheer him off the field, buy him beer afterwards, and finally pay a substantial match fee for the privilege.

No wonder then that mere ordinary mortals are continually having to make excuses for their conduct on or off the field. These range from almost genuine ones such as, 'It was your fault,' to classics of invention like, 'Just as he passed to me I remembered I had left the bath water running at home . . .'

The perfect rugby excuse should be as far away from the truth as possible. Rugby players, like other people, are given to fantasies, and if asked why you shirked a tackle, it is no use saying, 'Because I am a coward, skipper.' True this may be, but it will only earn abuse.

Whereas an outrageous lie, something like, 'My rupture was troubling me,' or 'The leg which I broke saving those children from a runaway horse gave way again,' will be accepted with only a grunt, and an exhortation to do better next time. Note that in the examples given, the blame is cunningly transferred to the captain, with the inference that he has abused a sick man.

A great deal of ingenuity is needed in making a good excuse, however. It won't work if you just blurt forth the first untruth that comes into your head. A player who concedes a penalty for offside is wasting his time if he says, 'It wasn't my fault. I was yards on. The ref's blind.' What is needed is something much more subtle, on the lines of 'Sorry, lads, but we all know this ref has hated me ever since I proved him wrong at Sidcup . . .'

That brings the skipper and the rest of the team on the side of the offender, so after the match they can use the same excuse, saying, 'We never had a hope. Charlie told us the referee has always had a down on us since he messed up that game at Sidcup last year . . .'

Thus the chain of fantasy goes on until a year or two later some perfectly innocent referee finds himself officiating at Sidcup and being greeted with snarls and hoots of derision for some reason he cannot understand.

Here then, are some suggested excuses to meet given situations:

On dropping a pass

'These damn contact lenses!'

'You may call it a pass but it looked like a dummy to me . . .'

'Didn't you hear me call "Scissors"?'

On giving a bad pass

'Poor Fred's eyes aren't what they used to be.'

'Poor Fred's hands aren't what they used to be.'
'Poor Fred isn't what he used to be.'

On refusing to fall on the ball

'I hate negative rugby. We want to open up the game, not close it down.'

On failing to win the strike in a set scrum

'I deliberately let them have the ball as a tactical move.'
'Fred put the ball at their feet. His eyes aren't what they used to be.'

On failing to score

'I injured my knee training last week. I always said strenuous training does more harm than good.'

On failing to turn up for training

'I injured my knee playing last week.'
'Standing for an hour in a tube train is harder exercise than running five miles.'
'All this training is making us stale.'

On being intimidated

'I did stand up to him. I told him to "— off" under my breath.'

On shirking a tackle

'I had my man covered. Maybe he didn't have the ball, but so what? Go for your own man is the golden rule. Fred should have got him.'

On failing to score

'Didn't you realize I was still blind in one eye after that match-saving tackle ten minutes before? Think yourself lucky I didn't leave the field.'

On everything

'The referee was a clot.'

'Look, I hate to keep mentioning this but you force me to remind you that I have a steel plate in my hip.'

CAPTAIN'S EXCUSES

On losing 48–nil

'It's that stupid fixture secretary. He ought to have known their winger once had a Scottish cap.'

On turning out with twelve men

'It's that stupid team secretary,' etc., etc.

On arriving half-an-hour after kick-off

'It's that stupid secretary of ours.'

On losing when he should have won easily

'No one will ever beat them as long as they have that touch-judge.'

'I would rather play clean and lose, than play dirty like them and win.'

REFEREE'S EXCUSES

On failing to award a perfectly good try

'Someone was standing in my way.'

'These contact lenses!'

'Try? What try?'

On disallowing a good mark

'My deaf aid isn't working very well.'

On playing forty-nine minutes in the second half

'The pavilion clock is wrong.'

'Why is there no pavilion clock?'

On not sending a player off for biting

'The skin wasn't actually broken, you know.'

On sending off the wrong man

'Well it may not have been him that time, but he deserved
   to go anyway. He's continually offending against Law
   14.'

For failing to warn a dirty player

'I looked at him severely.'

24

Fiona's Fab Time with the French

Hullo . . . hullo . . . is Penelope there? No, it's not Jonathan, it's me, Fiona . . . yes, Mrs Forsyte, I quite understand, Jonathan *does* have rather a high-pitched voice . . . well can you get her out of the bath? It's terribly important, I mean I want to tell her all about what happened to Rodney and me at the French match last week.

Hullo . . . Penelope, darling? It's *me*, Fiona. Yes, I know your Mummy thought I was Jonathan . . . well, this is about Rodney and me. We had a simply fab time at the French game last week. No, listen, darling, and let me tell you all about it.

Well, I must say I wasn't too keen on going with Rodney at first, because after that awful weekend when he was sick at the dance I've rather avoided him, but Taffy couldn't get stand tickets, and as he's been a bit off-hand recently I didn't mind when Rodney asked me to come.

Honestly, it was just *terrific*. We were in a gang along with the Old Rottinghamians. We had the most marvellous time at the City Barge and then we all drove off to Twickers, and Rodney had his Daddy's new Jag. His Daddy wants to wear it out so the firm will buy him a new one, so Rodney just drove it like a maniac. It was wonderful, especially when he carved up a 65 bus outside Kew Gardens.

Well, when we got to Twickers and parked the car we found that the Old Rottinghamians group were all next door to a pack of Frenchmen. Honestly, they were just a *scream*. They were all jabbering away to one another in some sort of foreign language . . . what? . . . yes, I suppose it would be French . . . and Rodney – honestly, this'll kill you – he went up to one of these Frenchmen and he said: 'Hey, why don't you — off, you Common Market thug?'

What's that? Yes, I had to whisper the first word. Well, Rodney said this to this Frenchman as bold as brass and the Frenchman simply smiled and nodded and said something in French, so do you know what Rodney did? He repeated very solemnly: '— off, you Common Market thug.'

And then, just to make it funnier, although by now we were all *baying* with mirth, he added: *'Oo lala, oui, oui, très bon.'* Well, honestly, at this stage, I just couldn't keep a straight face. I just had to do something or burst. Actually I burst. Anyway, that hook at the back of my bra broke suddenly. It wasn't so much what Rodney said, it was the way he said it, he kept a perfectly straight face all the time, but even Rodney started to giggle when one of the Old Rottinghamians suddenly shouted: 'You want my sister, *non*?'

Of course, all this time the French were just jabbering away to each other without seeing the joke at all. They just don't have a sense of humour like the English.

But that was only the start. The game? Oh, *that*. I gather it wasn't a very open sort. Actually, I wasn't watching all that hard because one of these Old Rottinghamians had got a banner he kept unfurling in front of my face. Rodney kept fairly quiet in the first half, mainly because he was busy explaining to me exactly what the players were doing wrong (Rodney sometimes plays in that funny position where you never pass the ball), but at half-time he just convulsed me.

I bet you'll never guess what he did. No, wrong . . . wrong again. I'll tell you.

He threw a toilet roll all over the crowd.

That was just the terminus as far as I was concerned. I just went back on my haunches and howled and howled and howled.

After the match, we were all in a bar and who should be there but the Frenchmen, each holding a glass of foam with a bit of beer at the bottom, and a sausage roll and they were looking at these and shaking their heads, just as if they thought the food and drink was poison or something. They kept muttering *'Ma foi'* or words to that effect. This inspired Rodney, who had us in fits all evening giving his imitation of Napoleon and when we got back home I asked him in for coffee. By a stroke of bad luck Daddy was still up, so Rodney, who was absolutely sozzled by now – he must have drunk three or four pints at least – went up to Daddy and pulled his funny face and spoke like a Frenchman and said: 'What am I?'

Unfortunately Daddy was in one of his beastly moods and he told him. I *hate* Daddy. But apart from that it was absolutely terrific. I wish we played the French every week . . .

25
Rugby and Religion

If a man is seen on his knees during a game of rugby it does not necessarily mean that he is unfit; he may well be praying. No other game in the world brings out such a deep religious streak as rugby.

The prayers are deep and fervent. The name of the Lord is continually invoked aloud, but the most sincere prayers are silent ones, delivered in the privacy of a heaving scrummage, and usually asking for mercy. Something like: 'O Lord, let this game end soon. I deeply repent me that I have been such a wicked person, especially as, judging by the way the blood is pounding in my ears, I may well drop dead on the pitch like old Charlie Jones did three years ago.

'O Lord, may I not drop dead on the pitch like Charlie Jones. May thy servant the referee be moved to blow his bloody whistle and end all this misery so we can get into the showers and after a few drinks get at the women, but if it would stop me dropping dead like old Charlie Jones then I am willing to give up the women this Saturday, O Lord . . .' This prayer is usually terminated by the worshipper realizing that the scrum is long finished and he is alone in the middle of the field on his hands and knees.

While prayers for the game to finish – whatever the result – are the most common (in sevens one can almost see them ascending in showers), there are several other forms, of which a favourite is the Prayer Maledictory.

In this, the Lord is asked to smite either the other side or some particular member of it. I know many older players who swear a good pray is more effective than a crash tackle. Perhaps on these lines:

'O Lord, let the whistle blow for a forward pass. But if in thine inestimable wisdom thou should decide not to perform this miracle, then let the dirty stinking rat put his foot into touch, and if in doing so he should break a leg, so much the better . . .'

The above examples are not the prayers of habitually religious people, but there is one large section of the rugby community whose prayers on the field are genuine, fervent and completely sincere – the Irish Catholics. When an Irish Catholic prays on the field, he doesn't do it furtively and silently, but rolls his eyes, raises his arms and calls to Heaven in a loud voice, 'O God, come down and blast the bastards . . .'

Not only does he really mean it, but he's quite convinced his plea has floated upwards successfully on the Guinness fumes, as any priest present would confirm. Having convinced himself his prayer must be heard he returns to the fray with renewed vigour.

Nonconformists are much less prone to prayer on the pitch, but plenty of them (especially the Welsh) like to indulge in sneaky prayers before the game, asking only that the Lord's will be done, especially if it happens to mean victory for their team. There was one famous Welsh international in the Thirties who before a big match always went into the local chapel and prayed, although I'm told his language if he missed a pass would have made a sergeant-major blush.

This idea that rugby and religion are somehow intermingled is not confined to the Welsh, of course. The Rugby Union itself always gives the impression that while the Devil invented Rugby League, the Lord chose the

Rugby Union as his own special game and probably referees occasionally in that greater Twickenham on High.

Perhaps this attitude is quite understandable in a game where the threat of serious injury or physical ruin is ever present, especially to the more elderly player. The beliefs (or lack of them) of the most confirmed atheist must begin to crack when he sees the opposition pack hurtling down upon him, or feels the pounding of the heart and constriction of the throat that precedes his half-time bout of retching.

It is a bold man then who can resist a rugby prayer.

26

How to Have a Happy Half-time

A cynic once suggested that rugby players don't leave the field at half-time because most of them wouldn't come back. It is, of course, forbidden without the referee's permission. Because of this, the rugby half-time, even at international level presents an odd contrast with that of the soccer clubs. While rugby players stand around steaming in the rain soccer men are resting in the changing-room and probably having egg-nog, oxygen and massage as well. They are also getting a thorough going-over from the manager whereas at least the rugby player is safely out of reach of officials.

A few players would prefer to do without half-time, as they say the rest makes them stiffen up but these are maniacs who should be ignored. For the average player, half-time comes as a golden couple of minutes of pleasure in an afternoon of unrelieved physical torture, and there are several ways in which he can make the most of this wonderful respite.

First, when the whistle blows, do not give way to the temptation to fall face downwards on the ground, gasping for breath or groaning feebly. This creates a bad impression on the skipper and encourages the other side. Try to stay upright, if necessary by limping to the goal and holding on to one of the posts.

If possible, ask the referee's permission to leave, since standing around in three degrees of frost hardly improves one's physical condition. I recall with great pleasure how I and a group of friends always used to go to the pavilion at half-time, ostensibly for a call of nature, but in reality to get into the boiler room and sit around on the hot pipes. The trouble was we used to lose all sense of time and they frequently had to send the full-back to fetch us. Or else we would return to find the team lining up to face a conversion while the captain shook his fist.

But leaving the field has its dangers. If you've had a bad first half, go off via touch-in-goal. Don't let any committee members have the chance to get near. Ignore anyone like the coach or chairman who beckons. If such officials should come on the field at half-time leave immediately in the opposite direction, despite any shouting or cries to return. Don't come back until it's safe to do so.

There is another danger in going to the pavilion. You might not have the strength to get back. I am not joking. I have seen an elderly player leave at half-time for a pavilion half a mile away at the other side of the playing fields. To save time he ran all the way there. When play was due to re-start we looked for him and saw his grey-haired figure wheezing towards us 800 yards away.

Everyone started waving and shouting and he broke into a shambling sort of trot but after he'd gone another fifty yards he had to sit down on a park seat to rest.

The referee wouldn't wait any longer so we started the game. Every time there was a stoppage we looked towards the pavilion and discovered the missing player moving towards us 100 yards at a time and stopping to sit down at every bench, where he would smile and wave feebly. He eventually arrived ten minutes after kick-off and explained he'd choked while trying to light a cigarette and run simultaneously.

Stranger still was the case of a player who picked up a girl on his way back from the pavilion. She was sitting on a seat with her dog and he bent down and patted the dog and then sat down beside her and started to chat her up. Of course, everyone was shieking at him to come back, but he just waved and smiled, and carried on talking.

By the time we kicked-off he was holding her hand. He didn't return until we sent a deputation to drag him back, and then he spent most of the game waving to her from the scrums and blowing kisses in the line-outs.

Sometimes it is not possible to leave the field. The main disadvantage of this, apart from the physical discomfort, is that one has to listen to the captain's half-time chat. The chief theme of this is false optimism about the side's prospects. Captains will never be honest and say, 'Well, lads, they're much better than us, we obviously haven't a hope, so don't bust your guts this half, save a little energy for the disco tonight.'

Instead, they go through the ghastly charade of pretending that it will all come right if everyone tries a bit harder. However, it is fatal to express disagreement with this codswallop. Nod occasionally and rub the knee as if an injury has been received. You may need the excuse later.

Finally, there is the referee, who during half-time normally stands alone, uneasily aware that both sides are looking at him and spitting. It is not a happy period for him but he must not weaken. The time can be put to good advantage by working out little problems, such as how to deal with that big forward who keeps obstructing, without sending him off.

One temptation the referee must resist at all costs: he must never be seen to drag out the RU Handbook from his pocket and start looking up the laws. If he wants to check what the penalty is for obstruction in in-goal, he should leave the field and do it secretly, preferably under his raincoat.

27

The Loneliness of the Long-distance Kicker

Some rugby statistician once worked out that 63 per cent of the points scored in the game came from kicking. My own view is that 63 per cent of the points scored are much more likely to come from cheating or the other team's mistakes, but that's another matter. What is certain is that although rugby is theoretically a handling game, it is still heavily slanted towards its football origins.

There are three different ways of scoring with a kick – a penalty, drop-goal, and a conversion. But there's only one way of scoring by running, and that is the try. And it's only thirty years since the drop-goal counted for more than the try. Indeed, originally a try counted for nothing and only the conversion scored. When points were first introduced in 1886 a try counted one point, and it didn't become three until 1894.

A stranger to the game, reviewing this situation, might well come to the conclusion that all rugby sides should concentrate heavily on improving their kicking and that the art would be a basic requirement, like passing.

He would, of course, be wrong. Proficiency at kicking is regarded as a gift from up above, which descends on only one man in the team, usually the full-back or stand-off. Any player who said at training he didn't want to practise passing, he'd prefer to try some kicking, would be hurled out on his ear.

When I was at school drop-kicking was absolutely banned. Once the First XV full-back, who later played for Leicester, dropped a goal in a fit of absent-mindedness and the effect was as if he had done something obscene. We all stared in horror while the rugby master hissed at him, 'You may consider yourself dropped from the First XV,' and I could almost swear he added the words 'miserable youth'.

Any boy who confessed to a desire to be a specialist kicker in those days would almost certainly have been told to take a cold bath every day, or whenever the evil desire overcame him.

Because a kicker is alone on the stage, so to speak, the penalties for failure are exaggerated. The groaning of 70,000 voices at Twickenham, all directed at one man, is terrible to hear. But at least top-class players are not usually abused by their own side. Down in the Extra B, the unhappy kicker is not only insulted by his team-mates but by the other side as well, who join in with cries of, 'Blimey, Vipers, you can't even score when it's handed to you on a plate,' and start pulling imaginary lavatory chains. Life can be hard for the unsuccessful kicker.

But perhaps the most terrible isolation of all is that of the man who can't kick and who makes a mark in the centre of the field, knowing he hasn't the skill to reach either touchline, even if he kicks at right-angles. This fear is best summed up in the immortal phrase of Tom Reid, Garryowen and Ireland: 'The deep and mortal dread of being found with the ball in me hands in the middle of Twickenham.' Except that the dread is equally deep and mortal on the Great West Road. No wonder the mark is unknown below third team level.

Because kicking is so neglected, most players are hardly aware of the subtle difference between the many types of kick, such as The Screw Kick, which floats into touch or curves infield at the vital moment. There are, however, different bad kicks which will be instantly recognizable.

The most common is The Hoop-la. This is frequently seen in suburban meadows, but is not unknown at Murrayfield or Twickenham. In this, the kicker steadies himself carefully, waits until the opposition are nearly on him and then meticulously, and with tremendous force, kicks the ball backwards over his own head. With luck, his own full-back may catch it, but more often the other side get there first.

Another frequently seen kick is, of course, the Non-Starter, in which the kicker misses the ball altogether. I've done it often myself and I don't know a more embarrassing thing on the rugby field. The worst of it is that the momentum of kicking swings you round and you fall flat on' your back while the ball bounces tantalizingly by your side, until some opponent seizes it gleefully.

Forwards seem to have their own special type of kick, The Grunt. It has always been a mystery to me why some sixteen-stone second-row forward, with legs like young oak trees, is only capable of feebly disturbing the ball when he has to kick it. Usually the ball travels in a tiny parabola for about three feet. You would think he'd be ashamed of himself, but oh dear no. After making a kick like this most forwards give a sheepish grin and go 'Huh, huh, huh,' to show that really they're not supposed to know how to kick and that it was jolly sporting of them even to try.

Place-kicking, too, has as many variations.

First, there's The Patella Fracture, in which the kicker stares mesmerized at the ball for some twenty seconds, slowly advances upon it and then buries the toe of his boot six inches in the soil about a foot in front of it. To make matters worse, he hops about on one leg voiding himself of yelps of agony, and may even retire from the field injured.

Then there's The Toppler. This isn't really a kick at all, since the ball refuses to stand up and be kicked. After the third time it falls over, the unhappy kicker is driven desperate by the jeers and groans of both sides and makes a wild stab at the ball as it lies at a drunken angle on the ground. Just occasionally, the ball actually goes over the bar, after describing a sort of corkscrew parabola. The effect on the opposition is dramatic and they are reduced to impotent silence, varied by occasional cries of 'Gawd', while the kicker pretends it was deliberate.

As one who has had the rare distinction of completely missing the ball in a place-kick, my own favourite variation is The Gurdoink, in which the kicker charges frantically at the ball, lifts his head at the last minute and scrapes his studs along the upper surface of the ball. Mercifully the laws have long ago been changed so the scrum-half does not have to hold the ball for a conversion, and the modern player is spared the sight of the ball skidding along the ground, accompanied by a piece of the scrum-half's ear.

I have referred to the isolation of the kicker, and in some ways his loneliness resembles that of a golfer. As for the golfer, there is the same necessity for a follow-through, for keeping the head down, for teeing up properly and for concentration at all costs. And like the golfer, the rugby kicker can be easily put off by some outside noise. True, first-class players become used to the storm of jeering which, alas, comes from many crowds. But there are more subtle forms of disturbance. A player who isn't at all put out by the entire Cardiff Arms Park hooting at him may well be put off by the sight of the opposing hooker sticking out his tongue. Worse still is the barracker (player or spectator) who makes a quiet but disturbing remark, just as you run up.

It's very difficult to put over a successful conversion when, as you stand to attention on the touchline, someone says distinctly, 'The police have just towed away your car.'

In lower sides the kicker may find himself subject to

somewhat cruder pressures, such as the entire opposition making funny faces at him. The shortness of the posts can be another hazard, since referees in this class of rugby invariably work on the principle that if the ball is kicked high over the posts, the side has cheated by inserting a First XV man, and the kick must be disallowed.

The home team may keep a special kicking ball on the touchline, which they produce for their own kicks, and then remove to its hiding place. Attempts to borrow this for an opposition kick will be met with physical violence, or in extreme cases the custodian of the special ball, usually the touch-judge, will curl up on the ground clutching it, and defy you to get it.

From a kicking point of view, I think the most extraordinary thing I encountered was a game on a park where we had no posts at all. It was one of those places where players have to put up portable posts, and there weren't enough to go around.

After playing for a short time with just a heap of coats where the posts should be we hit upon the ideal solution. Whenever a kick at goal was signalled we lifted up the posts and crossbar on the next pitch and carried them over. The kick was then taken, and the posts returned to their proper place.

The people on the next pitch were decent about it, and co-operated in every way. The only snag was that thanks to the continual delays, both games lasted for more than two hours, which is probably a world record.

28

The Day of Judgement

*(Although players always talk about
being sent off, comparatively few are,
and what happens at a disciplinary
committee remains a mystery, as their
proceedings are completely private.
However, from interviews I managed to
piece together what a typical hearing
might be like. Every single case is
authentic.)*

Sitting uncomfortably amid the discarded jock-straps of a
rugby changing-room are a group of middle-aged men.
The Loamshire Rugby Union disciplinary committee is in
session. (It should have met in a private room, but the
club got the dates mixed up.) The chairman calls the
meeting to order, and they hide their pints of beer as a
small, dark Welshman of about twenty-five comes in. The
chairman asks him: 'Is your name King Kong?'

'No.'

'But according to the referee's statement you gave your
name as K. Kong. Is that correct?'

'Well . . . my name is actually Jones.'

'Then why the hell say it was King Kong?'

'I must have done it in the heat of the moment.'

The chairman glances hopelessly at his colleagues, and
asks the player if he agrees with the ref's statement. His
reply will depend on whether the ref is present. If he is, the
player will probably express deep contrition. In this case
he isn't, so the defendant launches into a tirade of abuse,

accusing the referee of being blind, biased and incompetent.

Three witnesses from the team are called in support. All adopt a glassy expression, and repeat the same story word for word, asserting the innocence of the accused man and the idiocy of the referee. The chairman asks a test question:

'Was this in a line-out or scrum?'

The first witness says he thinks it was a line-out; the second knows it was a scrum; the third can't remember, but believes it might have been off the ball. So sentence is pronounced: another two weeks' suspension to the automatic four awarded for being sent off.

'Thank you, gentlemen,' mutters the now humbled player, cringing his way out of the room before muttering 'bastards' outside.

Next case. A long-limbed lout of about twenty, dressed in a T-shirt with an obscene slogan on the front, rolls into the room. On his forearm is tattooed the motto Death to My Enemies, plus a dagger. He is accused of kicking a player; trying to get the rest of his team to support him in throwing the referee into a nearby lake; and standing on the touchline chucking mud at the referee after leaving the pitch. He gave his name as John Thomas.

No witnesses are called, but the club chairman comes along to give evidence of the accused's character and plead for mercy.

'Basically, he is a very gentle sort of person,' says the club chairman, glancing at the defendant, who is fiddling with his trouser zip, and chewing gum.

'Yeah,' grunts the player, picking his nose.

'He is one of the best men we have. He must have been provoked.'

Despite his gentleness, the committee increase the suspension, and receive a torrent of abuse in return. 'I'll do the lot of you,' shouts the aggrieved player, 'especially that elderly geezer with the pipe.'

'Next please,' says the elderly geezer, unmoved, and a man of about thirty-five comes in.

He is only reprimanded, but tells the committee in a well-spoken way: 'I shall not take this lying down. As a solicitor, I know you have no rights in law to do this. I shall sue you all individually.' The committee members hide their grins. He is the forty-fifth man this season to threaten either to sue them or report them to Twickenham.

Most players take the verdict quietly. Many condemn themselves by loaded statements such as: 'He thrust his face against my boot,' or 'I may have jumped up and down on him, but it was purely accidental.'

Referees let themselves down too. One writes: 'On reflection, I would not have sent him off. I met him in the bar afterwards, and he bought me a drink and seemed a very decent sort of chap.' But it is too late for regrets. Simply by sending him off the referee has sentenced him to four weeks' suspension. The committee can only increase the ban.

Another man brings some of the opposing team as witnesses, and this time they do prove his innocence. They point out that after the accused had been sent off, the player who really threw the punch asked the referee if he could leave to have his injured knuckles treated. 'The ref was very sympathetic,' says a witness. 'He said, "What a nasty injury. How did you do that?"' But the committee cannot revoke the automatic suspension, merely see no black mark is recorded.

Most cases get a reprimand, or a few weeks' further suspension. A few may be suspended *sine die*, which for practical purposes means for ever. One veteran implores the committee for mercy. His wife could not stand the stain on the family name of his being banned eternally. So sentence is reduced, on condition he takes a solemn oath never to play rugby again. He does so.

One or two knotty problems emerge. A whole team is

reported by the captain of a cross-channel ferry for wrecking his vessel. They are suspended *en bloc*. A player was overheard alluding to the referee as an 'incompetent fart' on the way to the changing-room, and was 'sent off', although the game had finished. He claims this is illegal and the question is referred to Twickenham.

It is ten o'clock before the committee finishes its business. There is little competition to sit on it. Before the year is over it will meet fifty times, and already more cases have been heard than in the whole of last season.

29
Fit for Nothing

I feel sorry for the captain of the local rugby club. This is
the time of year when he issues last-ditch appeals for the
team to get themselves physically fit, messages couched in
the despairing language of a South American dictator
addressing the firing-squad before being liquidated.

These calls to arms are contained in a badly duplicated
and nigh-illegible newsletter (usually wrongly addressed),
and they run something like this:

'As you know, last season was one of the most disastrous
in the history of the club. Only five games were won out of
32 and we conceded no fewer than 568 points, scoring only
69, fifty of these from penalty goals. This record obviously
has room for improvement. The reason for our failure can
be summed up in exactly one word: The whole team just
are not fit enough.

'This year training will take place on Monday, Tuesday, Wednesday and Thursday, and I expect everyone to
be there. A five-mile run carrying lead weights will be
followed by sixty minutes of press-ups and a game of touch
rugby played with a medicine ball. No excuses for absence
will be accepted without a medical certificate signed by
two doctors.'

Brave words. But the reality is different. The last time I
attended such a training session (I was sneaking past the

ground on my way to the local boozer when I was dragged in) nobody turned up except the skipper and the two oldest members of the Extra B, who were earnestly discussing what they did in the Battle of Britain and gnashing their toothless gums. The captain and I did a few half-hearted exercises and then he sprained his ankle, which put him out of the game for five weeks.

Personally, I have always held the view that training in the conventional sense is dangerous and does far more harm than good. Not only is violent exercise bad for the heart but there is a grave danger of accidental injury while training. I need only refer to the dozens of England players who have lost their place in the national side through injury caused while training the day before the match. However, I used to have my own method of getting fit by following this simple programme:

AUGUST 2: Change to filter-tipped cigarettes.

AUGUST 8: Reduce smoking to forty a day.

AUGUST 14: Every day, when getting out of bed, lift right arm above head once, and let it fall slowly. Repeat with left arm. This makes the arm muscles supple.

AUGUST 18: Every day, sprinkle hands and face lightly with cold water on arising.

AUGUST 20: Drink a bottle of light ale every day on arising. This tip was given to me by a man with whom I shared a bed-sitter. The effect is astonishing. The palate is cleansed and the whole system toned up. My friend even continued the habit on his honeymoon.

AUGUST 21: Receive card for first trial. Burn it.

AUGUST 28: Ring up secretary and complain at not being picked for second trial. What do they think they are? As one of older members of club very hurt at being ignored. Have half a mind not to pay subscription, etc. etc.

SEPTEMBER 1: Pay last year's subscription.

SEPTEMBER 6: Play first game. Defeated 39–nil owing to

total unfitness of whole team, except skipper, who is fit but inefficient.

SEPTEMBER 7: Very upset. You train like mad and this happens. Revert to untipped cigarettes. Drop strict-training schedule, except for bottle of light ale in the morning. Threaten not to play again until rest of team are fit.

30

Rodney and the Stair Carpet

'Hullo, hullo . . . is that you, Penelope? Yes, it's *me*, Fiona. Yes, I know it's strange to ring someone up on your honeymoon night, but I've just got to tell you . . . Rodney can't do it! What's that? No, darling, he can do *that* – well, just, at any rate – but he can't come to the sevens with you and Jonathan next week. Why not? Darling, he's in prison. Yes, dear, that place where they put your Daddy after he smashed up the car . . . no, I'm not trying to drag up old wounds . . . Yes darling, it must have been positively grotty in Pentonville . . . well you see, it was all the result of the wedding. Yes, I know you couldn't be there. Yes, dear, we did thank you for the cake-dish. And everyone else who gave cake-dishes.

'It was all Daddy's fault really. He started drinking at dawn. I know he did because he got up early to make the tea and when I came down an hour later he hadn't even put the kettle on – he was just sitting by the radiator with a bottle of champagne. I asked him what he was doing and he said it was the happiest day of his life. No, dear, it was not a nice thing to say. He didn't mean it as a compliment.

'Well, honestly, by the time he came to take me to the church he was in a terrible state. He couldn't find his top hat anywhere and we had to go without it. Then he insisted on opening the car windows and shouting at people in the street. I don't know what the driver thought, but we got to what Daddy insisted on calling the "sacred edifice" all right, and Mummy and I got him inside by holding each arm, and I sort of led him up the aisle.

'And then we went through the ceremony and Rodney looked absolutely *monumental* in his morning-suit and it all went like a bomb until they came to that bit "with my body I thee worship" at which Daddy burst out into peals of drunken laughter and Mummy had to put her hand over his mouth to shut him up. The vicar looked outraged, especially as he hates Daddy ever since he took change for a pound from the collecting-plate. Then he loudly asked if there was any just cause or impediment and so forth, and of course there was complete silence, and in the middle of it all a Welsh voice muttered quite distinctly, "I should think there was," and I realized that awful creature Taffy Owen had got into the church. He was sitting with the rest of the Fourth XV at the back.

'Anyway, to cut a long story short, we got through it all (although I didn't like the way Rodney hesitated on "I do") and we marched out down the aisle and when we got outside there were the players with an arch of corner flags. It was wonderful. And then to my horror as we were marching under this arch I saw Taffy holding one of the flags and as we passed he said quite distinctly, "I've had her. And I didn't enjoy it." Honestly, I nearly *died*. And Rodney must have heard, because he got all sort of tensed up and he's always been jealous of Taffy but that's old history now.

'Well, anyway, off we went to the reception and Daddy was *beastly*, he kept slapping Rodney on the back and shouting, "Better you than me, old son," and pouring brandy into his champagne, and then he went over and actually shook Taffy by the hand, although he hadn't even been invited. I thought I was going to howl.

'Well, eventually we got to the speeches, and it was obvious by then that Rodney had been affected by

Daddy's champagne and brandy because instead of just saying a few words he went on and on and on. And then he started to become absolutely revolting and began making alleged humorous remarks like, "As a good forward I shall certainly push hard tonight," and then he told the most *obscene* story I have ever heard in all my life and Mummy's relatives' faces were going blacker and blacker and I just sat there frozen with horror. I was sure Uncle George was going to make a scene. Mercifully Rodney forgot the end of his story and Tubby Chapman, the best man, leapt up and thanked him and said he might be a joke as a full-back but he was sure he would find touch tonight, and they all howled with mirth and Daddy fell off his chair.

'Eventually Mummy and I had literally to drag Rodney away so we could change, and we were going to be driven in Tubby's car only when we got outside, it had been jacked up and all four wheels removed. So we went in Daddy's car (thank heavens Daddy refused to drive and Tubby did instead) and came back in Rodney's to say goodbye. Well, believe it or not it took another hour and a half to get Rodney away and a lot of it was Daddy's fault, he kept getting them together in a scrum and heeling someone's top hat. Eh? No, I don't know whose hat it was . . . Taffy's, I hope . . . but eventually we got away and drove off to the secret honeymoon hotel . . . no, dear, nowhere very exciting, Henley-on-Thames if you *must* know. Rodney had originally booked us in at Maidenhead but I made him change it. Well, there is a limit . . .

'Anyway, on the way, the most cataclysmic event occurred. A policeman stopped us on the motorway and asked Rodney if he was aware that he had a stair carpet trailing from the back of the car. They must have tied it on while we were waving goodbye. Well, to cut a long story short, the policeman got a sniff of Rodney's breath (not that that was difficult, you could have smelt the brandy five hundred yards away) and asked him to breathe into a bag and Rodney hiccupped and said he had a right to trail a stair carpet if he wanted, and the policeman said, "Not when it's got Star and Garter Hotel printed all over it," and then Rodney was rude to the policeman and the next thing I remember was sitting in the police station while they locked Rodney in some dungeon or other, and told me he'd come before the magistrate in the morning.

'So here's little Fionakins sitting in the bridal suite at Henley-on-Thames on her ownsome and all her friends imagining her revelling in an orgy of positive lust. No, dear, I don't intend to come back to London tonight. Can you imagine what Daddy would say if his own daughter rang the front doorbell on her honeymoon night? Besides, I've got to attend the trial or whatever they call it, tomorrow . . . and to think I voted for the return of flogging at the Young Conservatives . . .'

31

Eating Players is Wrong

The result of the introduction of 'new wave' rugby into Britain with its coaching, planning, team training and deep thinking, has been the virtual elimination of the extremes of physical and mental ability that used to characterize the average group of rugby players. Fortunately, the rot has not reached the Extra C, which will always be noted for the utter extremes represented by its players – seven-foot skeletons yelping pitifully on the wing, elderly dwarfs communicating in grunts during the line-outs. The appearance in such a motley crew of a new man who had never played rugby before, and who had to leave the field to adjust his truss, caused little surprise.

Today, even in the third team, it is difficult to hide anyone who doesn't know the rules. The days when a recruit from the local soccer club could be secreted on the wing are passing. What is the use of a winger who doesn't know what line-out signals are? And whatever has happened to that haven for older players, full-back?

I look back with pleasure on many an afternoon on some sodden field, leaning against the post and swapping jokes with the soccer goal-keeper behind me, while the Extra B battered away in the distance. Occasionally I would break away from my conversation to boot the odd ball into touch, before returning to resume the chat.

Indeed, an old friend claims that on one occasion he played full-back simultaneously for two teams who were occupying adjacent pitches, filtering from game to game as the situation demanded.

Today's with-it full-back, however, holds the busiest position on the field. When not in defence he's expected to be the spearhead of the attack and spends most of the afternoon following up his own kicks. It won't be long before you're too old to be a full-back at twenty-five.

From a physical point of view this means the end of the old full-back who was usually a pensioned-off fly-half of some thirty-five winters, still quite fast over five yards but otherwise moving at a gentle trot, and his replacement by a fervent lad who keeps complaining the threequarters can't keep up with him.

But nowhere has the change been more marked than at forward. Your old type of forward not only played differently from the backs, he looked different.

Front-row men had square bodies and heads, the latter occasionally coming to a point at the top. They moved on two stubby projections, and frequently on all fours. From time to time they emitted loud grunts and sometimes spoke simple phrases like, 'Why don't you — off, ref?' or 'I'll fix you at the next line-out.' They were not supposed to handle the ball at all, and if they did so their clumsy efforts would be greeted by roars of patronizing laughter.

Despite their strength, they had a habit of anticipating non-existent opposition, and on receiving a pass, had only one tactical move – they turned their vast posteriors to face the enemy, clutched the ball to their stomachs, and cringed. They would be quite capable of doing this ten yards from an undefended line.

Take Gnasher Brown, who said he used to play for Nuneaton, but who was shuffling around Victoria Park, Leicester, when I met him.

Gnasher had no teeth. But unlike most people, he had no false teeth either. A man of simple intelligence, he believed Nature's ways were best and ate with his gums, which over the years had become hardened to an incredible degree. This was, he told me, due to the example of his father, who had one leg. His earliest childhood memory was of his mother rubbing father's stump with turpentine to harden it, and the capacity of human flesh to harden into iron had impressed itself upon his mind ever since.

Besides eating with his bare gums, Gnasher used them on the field of play. Not to bite – he was a fair player, if rough. Gnasher actually used to tackle opponents with his mouth. Upon entering a maul, or loose scrum as it was called in those days, he would open wide and firmly fix his toothless jaw on the arm of some opposition player with such firmness the startled player would be rendered helpless.

Those who experienced his grip told me that apart from the vice-like hold, which would reduce a limb to tingling paralysis, the ghastly rubbery feeling of the gums induced a mental effect that caused a shudder every time the incident was recalled.

Once, a rather posh opponent complained to the referee that Gnasher had bitten him. The referee called Gnasher over and he strongly denied the offence, pointing out that it was impossible, as he had no teeth.

'Well in that case,' said the aggrieved opponent, 'he gave me a very nasty suck.'

Behind the old front-row used to be two lanky louts who formed the second-row of the three-two-three formation, and behind them were three slightly more literate louts who formed the back-row. The back-row were allowed to pass and run but were bitterly criticized for not pulling their weight in the tight if they overdid the open work.

I wonder what Gnasher would say to today's front-row forward, supposed to run, dummy, swerve and sidestep with the best of them. Not to mention clever tricks like long overhead passes and throwing-in at the line-out. Gnasher never passed in all his life. And any young forward who was so rash as to do so would receive his stern rebuke, 'Yo want to leave that sort of stoof to they bloody backs, kiddo . . .'

So much for the pack. What of threequarters, once the intellectuals of rugby, with a strong aversion to physical contact of any sort? They were delicate plants, frequently with university degrees, and usually from the upper or middle classes. Here the wheel has swung right round, and the modern back is now expected to scrummage, or at least invite the tackle and slip the ball back in the subsequent ruck. The result is that whereas the old-style threequarter looked like one with his creased trousers and his hair cream, today's backs all look like perfect second-row forwards.

Eventually we may see the development of an all-purpose player on the lines of the Fijian side, where the only difference between backs and forwards is that the forwards are faster. Soon every player will be able to run, ruck, scrummage, sidestep and drop-kick.

Mercifully, it is still impossible to conquer Nature completely. Down in the fourth team bald, square-headed men are still seen not only in the front-row, but in the threequarter line as well; arrant cowards, lily-livered youths and sexual deviationists still patrol the wings on countless public parks, and grandfathers are yet to be seen at prop forward. Long may it be so.

32

Spare My Blushes

There's a strange streak of masochism in rugby players. In most sports, people's favourite stories concern their successes but in rugby, failure is the favourite topic, and when I ran a competition in the *Sunday Times* for stories of humiliation the number of entries eclipsed those of any other similar competition, beating even the contest for referees' stories.

I kicked off by describing a humiliation of my own. Like so many rugby experiences, it didn't even happen on the field but took place on the London Road, Leicester, when I was playing for Leicester Thursday way back at the end of the forties. We had to carry our goalposts across the road from the Old Horse pub in those days and as I was staggering across the road I dropped the crossbar in front of a tram, which reduced it promptly to matchwood. The team collapsed with mirth while the tram-driver pursued me up the road. That simple yarn sparked off a flood of reminiscence in similar vein.

Surely the most bitter humiliation of all for a player must have been that experienced by the winger described by C. Blakey, of Wapping. During a massive defeat this unfortunate individual ran helplessly up and down the touchline for eighty minutes without ever once receiving the ball. When the match eventually finished, the referee came over and warmly thanked him for acting as touch-judge.

False teeth have played their part in many a story of rugby folklore, but a new slant came from Adrian Potts, of Coal Aston, Sheffield, who was playing on the wing outside a selfish centre. He became tired of never receiving a pass and when eventually a golden opportunity came he shouted desperately for the ball – so vehemently his false teeth flew out of his mouth. He stopped to retrieve them and the centre passed into empty space, costing a certain try.

Jerry Wellens, of Brixton, reluctantly taking part in a game at school, was shoulder-charged into touch by a player whom he described as 'the first-team psychopath, who loathed me.' Unfortunately he skidded into a field of sprouts by the side of the pitch, nobody noticed his absence, and he lay there semi-conscious until the match finished, when his groans attracted the attention of other players.

Perhaps the craggy wing-forward described by David Taylor, of Poulton-le-Fylde, Blackpool, was a psychopath, too. This aggressive individual became more and more frustrated at the lack of physical contact in a one-sided match. Near the end he received the ball with the line wide open but instead of running for it he deliberately headed for the opposing full-back, snarling at him. The full-back stared in disbelief and then fled towards his own line, zig-zagging frantically, as the savage flanker pursued him. The wing-forward caught him at the posts, felled him with a savage blow, and dived over for a try.

Captains naturally featured quite a lot. The skipper and three men from Reading Wanderers, for instance, arrived late at an away match to see the opposition kick a penalty goal against eleven men. At half-time the captain fiercely harangued the side. 'We're only three points down, we can still do it if we try,' he shouted, banging his fist into his hand, until someone pointed out they were in fact leading 4–3, having scored a try before he arrived.

Edward Young, of Chinnor, wrote of a captain who raised his fist high to emphasize a point in a pre-match pep talk – and crashed it through the window behind him. They played one short while he went to hospital.

Another skipper, Godfrey Hurley, of Bridgend, captain of the local Railway Inn, also had to go to hospital for stitches after sustaining a nasty gash in a game. But it wasn't during play, it was trying to cut up the half-time oranges with a blunt penknife . . .

Unusual injuries played a bit part in many stories. Bill Wanley, captaining Old Coventrians Second XV, led them in such a savage warm-up that he collapsed with a torn muscle and had to be carried off the pitch before the game had even begun. And John Shaddard, of Weston Turville, told of the Wasps hooker who returned from a game in the West Country with fifteen stitches in his backside. He hadn't even played – he sat down on an empty pint mug in the clubhouse.

Even a touch-judge can be injured. J. Miles, of Rugby, ran the line after quitting as a player and, anxious to make a good impression in an important game against mighty Coventry, he trotted on the field with the team so smartly that he pulled a leg muscle and had to be carried away on a stretcher, to the jeers of the Coventry crowd. To make it worse, one of the bearers was laughing so much he dropped the stretcher.

David Clipsham, playing for Newark Fourth XV, made what must be the shortest appearance ever in a match. He tried to mark the ball direct from the kick-off, and dug his heel in the ground so ferociously that he twisted his ankle and had to be helped to the touchline.

Being hauled off the field by the police was the humiliation suffered by a Scottish Border League player. Apparently he skidded on a snow-covered road on his way to the match, abandoned his car in a ditch and walked to the match. The police found the car, traced him, and stopped the game to escort him from the field for a breath test. It proved negative – and he returned to play out the match.

Among the stories was one from a girl player, Henrietta Crudas, of Newcastle, who described a ghastly insult to her femininity when playing for a men's side against a female team in a pub sevens. There was a rule men could not tackle or hand off women. Henrietta thought it did not apply to her and handed off an opponent, whereupon the referee awarded a penalty. 'But ref,' shouted her side, 'she's a girl.' The referee peered closely at Henrietta's bosom and after a long inspection said, 'Well, it's still a penalty in my opinion.' As Henrietta commented, 'Back to the chest-developing exercises!'

A charming Irishman I met in Edinburgh alleged he was skipper of Bective Rangers G XV (that seems a humiliation for a start). 'I used to captain the F XV but I got out of condition,' he said sadly. He told me a story of embarrassment in a remote part of Ireland, when an opposition player was ordered off in a rather fierce game. Unfortunately he was the owner of the only ball. 'If I am sent off I shall take my ball with me,' he said, and suited action to the word. End of game.

Another Irishman (or perhaps he was the same one looking blurred – it was one of those evenings) said he was playing in a match in which a player kicked a ball into touch so hard that it vanished over some park railings into a locked area. The referee ordered the offending player to fetch the ball. He refused. 'Either get the ball or get off the field,' boomed the referee. With a snort of defiance, the player marched off the field. Soon afterwards everybody else followed him, since it was the only ball and the railings were unconquerable.

Half-time was the occasion of embarrassment for Mike Parkinson, of Sandal, Wakefield. It was his first game for the First XV of his local club and he was desperately anxious to impress. At half-time an angry captain was sounding-off at the players grouped around him on the pitch when Mike heard someone whisper 'pssst' behind him. He turned round to find his grandmother and grandfather had ambled on to the middle of the field. They handed him a bag of unpeeled oranges and told him, 'Hand these round to your friends,' and then wandered off again, leaving a young player scarlet with shame and a team in fits of laughter.

One person who wrote in was an old mentor of mine, Alan Rees, of Garnett College, London, who tried to teach me psychology when I was a student there. He recalled the time at a Welsh university when he was conscripted as touch-judge by the rugby side for an important away game, after travelling up with the table-tennis team. However, he managed successfully until there came a critical conversion by the other side which would settle the result. The ball just floated the wrong side of the post and Alan leaped into the air, waving his flag in ecstasy – and the referee assumed the conversion had gone over. His explanation: 'Well, I'm really with the table-tennis team,' became a legend at his university.

Two whole teams were involved in one unfortunate experience. The famous Bristol club, Clifton, were playing a Second XV game with Trowbridge and both sides lined up for a minute's silence before the game in respect to the dead, only to find out they were paying a last tribute to someone's cat. The animal belonged to John Hickey, usually First XV full-back, who had been irritated at the lack of sympathy shown by team-mates at the death of the pet, so he decided to get his own back and told the referee that a valued member of Clifton had died and could they have a minute's silence before the game.

Afterwards he tried to collect money for a wreath, but no one would contribute.

Young people take things seriously, and Gerry Davis, of Ilford, described an experience which proved too much for a sensitive seventeen-year-old playing for East-hamians Fourth XV. He was about to score the first try of his life when a stray dog appeared on the pitch and barked furiously at him and the pursuing full-back. The full-back retreated in fright and the youth was able to touch-down. But just as he was overjoyed at his success the referee ran up and disallowed the try because one of his side had encouraged the dog to attack the full-back by shouting, 'Seize him, boy, kill, kill,' which the referee said consti-tuted ungentlemanly conduct. The young winger was so disappointed he never played again.

One of the craziest stories related came from Geoffrey Broad, of Leigh-on-Sea. Playing for Old Westcliffians he went to field a high ball at the same time as a colleague and got his studs entangled in the other player's laces. 'Both of us were inextricably linked in a three-legged race complete with rugby ball,' he said. Meanwhile the op-position pounded towards them. Eventually they threw the ball into touch, as the only way of saving the situation.

Graham Morrison, of Darris Hall, Northumberland, thought glory had come when they picked him for the county under-21. He psyched himself up in the dressing-room and was just snarling and beating his chest in the approved style when the captain asked, 'Do you always play in glasses?' He threw them aside in shame and thundered on to the field. But the changing-rooms were at the end of the ground and he ran straight into a goalpost. 'I wasn't picked again,' he said.

Warwick Shipstone, of Wanlip, Leicester, also ran into a post. But he had his eye fixed on a huge twenty-stone opponent who was about to pulverize him, and didn't look where he was going. Suddenly there was a bang and he found himself on the ground, temporarily paralysed.

M. J. Melody, of Cleckheaton, recorded the plight of a man whose wife mended his torn shorts and forgot to remove the pins, a fact he discovered during his first run, which ended in shrieks of pain.

There was a charming letter from B. D. Harding, of Norwich, which proves how diverse are the types of people who play rugby and how wrong is the stereo-typed image of the beer-swilling hearty. 'In the late 1960s I was playing on the left wing for Old Dunstablians at Biggleswade,' he wrote. 'The game was nearing no-side and we were trailing by a single point. A movement started in our twenty-five and eventually reached the Biggleswade twenty-five. At this point we had an overlap with our centre needing only to draw the full-back and pass to me for an easy run in. Here starts the humiliation. I have been interested in birds (*aves*) ever since childhood. Along the side of the pitch was a stream and at the very moment the ball was passed in my direction a Grey Wagtail called. This attracted my attention and my next recollection is of the ball flying past and bouncing straight into touch. You can imagine the comments of the rest of the team . . .'

Yes, I can. Incidentally, Mr Harding's interest in birds took him to Siberia in 1982, and the hotel barman may still be wearing the Norwich RFC pullover he gave him.

And another nature story from Bill Thompson, who used to be a great man in RAF rugby. He claimed that he once held up a game at Abingdon to pick some mushrooms on the pitch. To add insult to injury, he asked the referee if he could borrow his handkerchief to hold them . . .

Probably the most unusual – and gruesome experience – was that of John Summerskill, of Halifax, whose story reads like a script from a horror film. During a very rough game he went to retrieve the ball from a cemetery beside the pitch and found that it had landed on his own family tomb. To make it worse, his own name was glaring from the gravestone, and repeated several times, as the eldest son is always called John. He returned to the match deep in thought and spent the rest of the game trying to avoid getting hurt in any way.

Blackheath's Peter Piper, who played for the club's

lower sides when President, still finds that old age brings a permanent humiliation to him. 'I wear the leg parts of my wife's tights so as to reduce the agony of pulling out hairs when I unstrap my legs,' he wrote, 'and I also have one of her girdles round my chest to protect my elderly, cracked ribs.' No wonder newcomers eye him with suspicion in the dressing-room when he stands there clad in ladies' underwear.

Humiliations of English sides by the Welsh are nothing uncommon, but Michael Perkins, of Alcester RFC, told of one that must cap the lot. His team played against Garndiffaith, near Pontypool, on the morning of an international, with four inches of snow on the pitch. The Welsh, who won 48–0, were so confident of victory they actually built a snowman inside their own twenty-five!

Even when you hit success some accident can make it all look silly. As when Old Beccehamians won the *Rugby World* Team of the Month award. A photographer and reporter arrived to present it, but as the ground was unfit the match was transferred to a new venue. Play had already started when the magazine officials arrived but at half-time they came on and took photographs and made the presentation. This delighted the team as it was the Old Boys Sixth XV, who were not used to winning anything. Meanwhile, on a field six miles away, the First XV waited alone and in vain . . .

The winning entry came from Jeremy Cartland, of Brighton, for an experience of the deepest embarrassment.

'The use of a white ball and the fact that I am bald combined to give me my most humiliating experience,' he wrote. 'Playing in mud and pouring rain our scrum was being pushed back over our line. As the ball squirted back from the scrum I gratefully fell on it for a twenty-five drop out. The opposing scrum-half, cross at being outwitted, jumped on me and pushed my face in the mud. At this point the referee arrived from the other side of the scrum, saw my bald head being pushed into the ground, thought it was the ball, and awarded a try . . .'

I feel that combines all the true elements of Coarse Rugby – a bald player, an ill-tempered opponent, a bog of a pitch and a short-sighted referee. What more fitting note on which to end?

BESTSELLING HUMOUR BOOKS FROM ARROW

All these books are available from your bookshop or newsagent or you can order them direct. Just tick the titles you require and complete the form below.

☐	THE ASCENT OF RUM DOODLE	W. E. Bowman	£1.75
☐	THE COMPLETE NAFF GUIDE	Bryson, Fitzherbert and Legris	£2.50
☐	SWEET AND SOUR LABRADOR	Jasper Carrott	£1.50
☐	GULLIBLE'S TRAVELS	Billy Connolly	£1.75
☐	THE MALADY LINGERS ON	Les Dawson	£1.25
☐	A. J. WENTWORTH	H. F. Ellis	£1.60
☐	THE CUSTARD STOPS AT HATFIELD	Kenny Everett	£1.75
☐	BUREAUCRATS — HOW TO ANNOY THEM	R. T. Fishall	£1.50
☐	THE ART OF COARSE RUGBY	Michael Green	£1.95
☐	THE ARMCHAIR ANARCHIST'S ALMANAC	Mike Harding	£1.60
☐	CHRISTMAS ALREADY?	Gray Jolliffe	£1.25
☐	THE JUNKET MAN	Christopher Matthew	£1.75
☐	FILSTRUP FLASHES AGAIN	Peter Plant	£1.25
☐	A LEG IN THE WIND	Ralph Steadman	£1.75
☐	TALES FROM A LONG ROOM	Peter Tinniswood	£1.75
		Postage	
		Total	

ARROW BOOKS, BOOKSERVICE BY POST, PO BOX 29, DOUGLAS, ISLE OF MAN, BRITISH ISLES

Please enclose a cheque or postal order made out to Arrow Books Ltd for the amount due including 15p per book for postage and packing both for orders within the UK and for overseas orders.

Please print clearly

NAME ....

ADDRESS ....

....

Whilst every effort is made to keep prices down and to keep popular books in print, Arrow Books cannot guarantee that prices will be the same as those advertised here or that the books will be available.